ALL SHALL
BE WELL ...

ROBERT GRAHAM

with Richard Carr, Helen Cross, Elizabeth Porter & Graham Tyrer

All Shall Be Well...

By Robert Graham

ISBN: **978-0-9559053-0-8**
Published by Purflain Press

First Published 2008
Copyright© Robert Graham

Produced by **Wright's Printers Ltd.**
9 (old) Middlewich Road, Sandbach Cheshire CW11 1DP

Contents

"Throughout those meditative, slowly uncurling, tactful and quietly excited sentences,

there is a vivid awareness of possibility; of fresh and further understanding,

and in that sense they are unfinished without being at all raw"

Foreword

This book originated in the 1990s as a response to the accumulating evidence that much was wrong in the world of education. It was conceived not as a negative rant or as an attempt to offer easy solutions but rather as a search for understanding. Robert Graham who had recently retired from teacher training brought together friends and former students from the Durham University PGCE to produce a book which is full of insight and inspiration. In contrast to much contemporary writing on education which is formulaic and bland, this work is original in its conception and style, and full of challenging and engaging content. The authors were each invited to write about the world of education as they experienced it, without being constrained by any predetermined structure or narrow starting point. The diversity of the resulting chapters is part of their overall appeal. The book has succeeded in attaining the 'inner coherence' that Robert Graham had hoped for and to which he makes reference in his introduction. As well as sharing a common vision, the chapters have several features in common. Each one uses honest reflection on experience as its starting point so that the general insights are rooted in concrete examples that readers will recognise and some will share. All of the contributors are accomplished writers who are adept at using metaphor and literary allusion to convey the subtleties of their understanding. They all write in a way which invites dialogue and reflection without closing off possibilities. Robert Graham died in 2001 before this project was completed. His own chapter in which he reflects on his illness and uses that experience to inform some of his most penetrating writing makes particularly poignant reading. He was an inspirational teacher and mentor, and full of wisdom, a virtue that is insufficiently valued in our times. He would have been delighted to see the book's publication in the hope that readers might find encouragement, support and learning from its content. It is sad that he did not live to see that happen but the book is a fitting tribute to his memory and will both challenge and enrich its readers.

Michael Fleming
Durham University

Introduction: Robert Graham

The idea for this book came to me in the mid-1990s. I had retired from full-time work as a teacher trainer some seven or eight years earlier. During the next few years a good deal came my way in connection with the world of education, and indeed the world itself, from ex-colleagues and past students, and through the media, that was decidedly disturbing; yet no one seemed to be able to do much about it. I kept thinking of what the young firebrand, and later much honoured Cardinal, John Henry Newman had written in 1833 in the first of the notorious **Tracts for the Times**, which he and friends circulated vigorously around the country. *"Yet speak I must," he wrote, "for the times are very evil and no-one speaks against them."* The words had a splendid ring. You couldn't write things like that, these days, though, could you. *"Very evil"*? Hardly the language of the clear-sighted, enlightened 1990s.

All the same there did seem to be a lot going badly wrong, certainly in my old profession. So many people going off work with stress, or stress-related illnesses. I had known of the odd person being off work, or even disappearing completely, under sometimes slightly mysterious circumstances, during my own time as a teacher, but very seldom. And all those older teachers, what was making such a lot of them, most surprisingly the ones who had reached the top of the tree, look so eagerly for early retirement?

Occasionally particular signs of the times came my way. A really decent man I had known for years, the sort I would have most happily trusted children of my own with, was hounded into illness and months off work by his headteacher, and no one seemed able to do anything to help. The pretext for persecution was simple, an inspection by the Office for Standards in Education (Ofsted) had decided in its breezy manner that the snapshots, so to speak, which they had taken of the school did not fill them with total satisfaction, and nor did those they had taken of him. The predictable, though not of course inevitable, consequence? – the release of scapegoat hunting into the world, and an attack of what I have called elsewhere the Noah Claypole Syndrome – if pecked yourself, pick someone below to peck, and do it good and hard. This couldn't have happened in my time, not so brazenly and unopposed. Not that the urge to hunt out scapegoats was anything new, just that opportunities for it to emerge and exercise itself were not so invitingly made available.

Then there was the evening with the married couple, old friends from choral singing days, both Primary School Deputy Heads now and just the sort of people children need about them. There they were, sitting on the settee in our lounge, describing how they had worked out that if they both retired within the year, which they longed to do (both were in their early 50s), they could just scrape by until eligible for their pensions.

There were letters from past students also. Here for example, an extract from a letter written by a highly gifted man, already in a senior position in a secondary school. He comments on the way in which the world appears to be viewing teachers,

> "It seems that the idea of Education has been so consistently abused and hijacked that 'teacher' has become an all-purpose, umbrella word like union, fascist, Trotskyite, etc. etc.: the late 20th century English equivalents to Robin Goodfellow or Machiavelli. And there's no logic to it. We're raging lefties **and** we're old-fashioned, boring bastards in elbow patches; we've a cushy life with long holidays **and** we're idiots to work so hard for so little financial reward."

It wasn't exclusively other people's experiences that were coming my way. There was, for example, the great heap of paper that fell on my desk a few weeks before I retired, a sufficiently short time before, fortunately, to allow me to leave it abandoned in the eternal pending tray. It wasn't that I thought I ought never to have to give an account of myself and my work, rather that the extent of creative accounting and hoop jumping required to enable me to satisfy the demands of this lot was a wretched prospect indeed, to say nothing of the evident fact that my previous three decades in the business had nothing whatever to contribute to any judgments that might be made about me. It is certainly not my impression that since those days, in my old job at all events, demands for creative self-justification have diminished, in either extent or frequency.

Life as a Tutor for the old Marriage Guidance Council, just then turning itself into Relate, was starting to be haunted by requirements of a similar kind too. If we couldn't come up with some pretty precise ways of measuring and quantifying our efficiency and effectiveness, as purveyors of that phenomenon called Counselling, then we'd better think harder. The Age required such techniques, ergo such techniques there must be.

We had been told of course some time before that there was no such thing as society; furthermore, we must all surely know that, whatever else might or might not be the case, one truth at least could be relied on – Economics *was* the bottom line, and, as if to prove it, the Berlin Wall had fallen down. It was thus plain for all to see that we *did* live in a mighty Market Place, and woe betide anyone who tried to buck the market.

Everyone had a product to sell and customers to satisfy. And that meant everyone: teachers, doctors, nurses and counsellors; lion tamers, management consultants, spin doctors and stuntmen. Everything had its price tag; and if the product wasn't worth its price, have no fear – the customers might still be willing and happy to pay, but the quality control men would get you in the end.

"Thoughts of a dry brain in a dry season." Those final words of T S Eliot's ageing Gerontion were often in my mind too. It wasn't my world any more anyway, at least not the education part of it; let it be. So there they were, those two possibilities, the young man's passion to expose evils, the older one's weariness with them. Yet each possibility in its way impossible. Around that time, though, something being blazoned forth as the Third Way was coming into fashion. Maybe there might be a third way for me too, a way that would be more to do with finding out what I really did think about these things, and what some others too, for whom I had a high respect and regard, might think. It would certainly be a lot more interesting (if more difficult) than clarion prophecy or gloomy resignation, and probably a good deal more entertaining too.

I wrote to four past postgraduate certificate of education students, all variously in mid-career and mid-life now, and all people who, over the years, had become friends. I thought they might be interested in the idea of us trying to write a book together, and indeed they were. Since then one of them had to drop out because of the press of other work, and I invited two others to join the project. After outlining some of my own feelings about the times we were living through, I suggested that if we each took the time to find out and write down, at whatever length and in whatever way seemed appropriate, what it was we *really* had to say from our very different standpoints, then we might produce a book not only well worth reading, but also one that might have a powerful inner coherence without our needing to impose an unhelpful structure on it at the start. Such a project ought to be of great value to each of us, but we should only set about it if it sounded exciting and of the greatest interest as well.

We met for a couple of days early on, and since then have exchanged ideas and drafts through the post, and met occasionally (all or some of us depending on time and circumstance) to read and comment on what we have written, always in the hope of liberating rather than limiting our own and each other's thinking.

It is four years ago now since I suggested in the original proposal, expansively as I thought, that we might give ourselves a whole year for the project. We trust that taking the time we actually needed will have improved the outcome; our faith and interest have certainly never flagged. The reward has been in the doing. If our various writings, however, find readers who enjoy them, and feel supported and even renewed by them, or find their own thinking encountered and encouraged, and even vindicated and enriched, we will be happy indeed to be so additionally rewarded. It has always been our belief that we live and work amongst countless others who are also profoundly affected, not to say distressed and angered, by the arrogant and crude over-simplifications, the needless cruelties, dare one say the evils of the age. If what we have to say speaks to any of these many others, we hope that it supports and encourages them too, to have their say and make their stand, and provides a comfort and support to those who are already doing so, yet who may sometimes feel their struggle to be a misunderstood and lonely one.

'All Shall Be Well'...
Robert Graham: A Memoir

by Richard Carr

Bob Graham died on the 3rd of August 2001, in the Newcastle hospital where his admired Wittgenstein once worked. So shortly did his death occur after the completion of his work for this volume that these words of his might look like a valediction, a kind of final distillation of his thinking; Bob certainly knew, perhaps before his doctors, that he was dying. But how unvaledictory those words are... throughout those meditative, slowly uncurling, tactful and quietly excited sentences, there is a vivid awareness of possibility; of fresh and further understanding, and in that sense they are unfinished without being at all raw. Finality was not something Bob believed in.

Bob's early years, in a not particularly well-off middle-class family, his education at a minor public school, his immediate and lifelong devotion to music, his schoolday prowess as a runner, his wildly comic national service, his years as schoolteacher, university tutor in literature, counsellor and educationalist, - I shall say little about these, because I know little, and what I do know is only a faint background to our relationship. His personal qualities, huge appetite for friendship, some of the recurring themes in our conversation over seventeen years, these are more to the point. Bob, I think, in contemplating his early life, thought about it primarily as a set of promptings to reflection and as a seedbed of treasured relationships through the decades.

The first quality Bob manifests in my memories of him is an unquelled interested optimism: 'All shall be well...', in the words of Julian of Norwich he cites in his last pages. Bob was incapable of lack of interest – even things that left him cold interested him in coldness and the reasons for it. The cancer that killed him, at the far too early age of 64, was not uninteresting to him: he knew all about it, even while he was being reassured that it was pneumonia. He knew how he wanted to be treated. He knew the infuriating difficulty of performing hitherto minor tasks when ill, and the way that illness, like a spotlight switching on from an unconsidered corner, forms unfamiliarly-angled shadows, an unsought perspective. He knew all this because making sense of things without claiming to have exhausted them or solved them was the way his optimism worked.

'Making sense of things' in a quietly determined, yet unemphatic, manner is a very Bob-like characteristic. Though he knew a lot, he never professed answers or

solutions. He 'knew' that knowledge could only be, or not be, fruitful, and that knowledge at its most valuable was a form of respect, not of pride. And only more living answered the problems of living. For a man so closely associated with teaching, counselling and thinking about teaching and counselling, it is to say the least of it, striking that he did not try to teach people things. In seventeen years' close friendship I do not recall anything akin to teaching – no coaching, instruction, tricks of the trade, judgment, assessment. He would try to help, certainly, if one needed help, and some students of his needed help at two in the morning, or in the middle of a dinner party. What Bob did instead was open perspectives, suggest or exemplify unsuspected ways of coping or beginning to reflect upon situations. Until he did so, and one caught on to what he was up to, few students, I should think, would have experienced such a vital and encompassing version of the ambiguous activity of 'teaching'. Solutions of any kind, including those we would meet later in our careers under titles like 'development planning' or 'action planning', suddenly seemed bare, thin and weak. Teaching for Bob, then, was a form of being: it was this which let his optimism work on others.

Bob sometimes made claims about what he was not that support this unemphatic and liberating optimism. He claimed not to be a competent literary critic, for instance. He was thoroughly trained in and respected the academic virtues, of course (one way in which he respected Buber's I-It relation as well as the I-Thou), but simply refused to be regarded as an expert. He hated the idea, common among inexperienced students, that expertise, signalled by academic letters, unlocked secrets and treasures. To Bob treasures were always nearby and accessible: a Wittgensteinian perspective and a good example of his optimism. What counted instead was richness of relation to what one read as well as to whom one met or loved.

When I met him as a student of his in 1984 I felt immediately that he was something new in my experience – an academic tutor with a grave distrust of some forms of the academic enterprise. To Bob richness of relation could actually be decreased by academic habits and position: the rich consideration of a question could be masked by 'reviewing the literature', by research, by conferences, by discussion of competing positions. At bottom, the whole notion of merely competing positions struck Bob as a silly, vain game that evaded the I-Thou perspective and worked against optimism. In the words of a schoolfellow of his, "He was the only person I've ever met who actually read and loved the 'great' literature that intellectuals and academics are so dryly knowledgeable about."

The second great quality I associate with Bob is his trustworthiness, and it is linked with his optimism and his modesty. Bob's writing shows this. His relaxed, meditative style, occasionally tautening and always moving with a certain sense of its own liberty, has an instinctive tact, and that tact is a kind of strength. I mean by this that Bob knew well how to touch on a topic without letting it draw his line of thought astray, and without tamely following its complexity into some inextricable tangle. The rhythm and clarity of his style are effects of this restraint. But, equally, this meditative tact allows his writing to display the unfinalised optimism visible elsewhere in his life. His cast of mind was strong enough, that is, to be receptive and not to try to bend the objects of his thought to his will; not to be anxiously expert or definitive.

Modesty about his expertness and the wiry restrained modesty of his style are not simply modesty, therefore. They express a moral and aesthetic purpose, a certain steel in Bob's character that was essential to him and made him, for so many people, utterly and profoundly trustworthy.

Though I have thought a good deal, since his death, of what Bob meant to me intellectually, I keep coming back to seemingly simple qualities like 'trust' and 'optimism' because, I think, in Bob I saw them working to produce seemingly unsimple events like surprising and delicate discriminations or dazzlingly clear glimpses of tangled complexities. The contrast in Bob between his attentiveness to the minute and everyday, and his marvellously sharp manoeuvring in the rarefied air of philosophy or psychology, therefore, isn't an actual contrast at all. Bob's mind operated with equal wholeness and aliveness at all mental levels, and it is that which allowed his optimism and trustworthiness to work up and down the whole spectrum of mental activity.

His conversation and even his physical presence had a remarkably tonic effect because of this. In person he was long, rangy, white-bearded from his fifties, and in personality gently-spoken, deep-voiced but capable of an unnervingly wild, reedy, round-eyed laugh. He had brilliant grave blue eyes that, at the very moment he was encouraging you flippantly not to take him seriously, could flash deep into yours and you took him entirely seriously. He was not judging your ability to understand him or assessing the depth of your agreement, but alive with hope that your two perspectives might meet and merge for an instant. The tonic effect of his presence came from such moments. It made him more friends, of every degree, than anyone I have ever known. His students tended to keep in touch with him because they were able to feel the hope, the trust, the fruitful space Bob created between them, and they, like Bob, delighted in such contact.

Everything about Bob's conversation was spacious and various. It was as if the full range of conversational possibilities were suddenly present (remember those 'nearby and accessible treasures'). Humour, anger, puzzlement, enlightenment, speculation, confession, information, reasoning, remembering, interpreting; all were part of any Bob conversation. Seriousness and absurdity blended and separated and blended again quickly and easily. In a single evening Bob could range over Schubert, self-help books, Victorian houses, beer, Wittgenstein, different ways to bowl a leg-break, Vienna, the German language, Jake Thackray, Fritz Wunderlich, sand-wedges, the counselling industry, 1950s graffiti, the 'chapel mentality', things you wish you hadn't said, ectoplasm, GK Chesterton, cannabis, postmodernism and aubergines. I know because I was there.

The words used so often in this book – like 'encounter', 'uncertainty', 'reality' – are Bob's words. They express something of the ultimacy of Bob's thought, and around them has gathered a good deal of what we have come to think. They're puzzling, indeterminate, yet compulsory words, about which one has to think if one thinks at all. But they're not words an inexperienced writer, no matter how clever, would take as starting-points. You won't come across them in the pub very often, nor perhaps in PH.D theses. They might strike some as 'highbrow' or 'academic' but they won't strike many academics as such. In conversation with Bob they were natural, and though we might have used them without much attention since we began to think, they have through our contact with Bob and each other been, in a sense, naturally selected. They have become magnetic.

Bob has certainly, then, influenced us, his students and friends, but it's the bits of us that are most really ourselves that have responded most to his example. I think Bob might have been amazed, at an earlier stage of his life, that he could become influential. He was certainly aware of his qualities, but first, he was grateful for them because they opened up life to him, and secondly, he never completely left behind more perplexed or anxious Bobs earlier in his life, and would not have wanted to. His projected next book would have been about them and how they learned to expand, for expand they did, into the deeply interested, loved, generous man we know, with his own unexpected but rewarding manner of thought, a man original in himself and one who radiated a great and exemplary humanity.

Hard Times for Humanity
Some thoughts on how we meet each other these days

by Robert Graham

I begin by suggesting what seems to me to be the relative unawareness in contemporary society of the presence and possibility, in Martin Buber's terms, of the Primary Word Ich-Du, I-Thou, and in particular an unawareness in relation to it that seems to pervade the spheres of the world with which I am most familiar, especially the educational. There is nothing original in this idea but I think that any opportunity to express and explore it is worth taking. My own expression and exploration of it is going to be an essentially personal one; most of what follows comes out of my own experience and that of people in various ways close to me. I don't apologise for that, indeed I will take a great name in my support and suggest that this is one of those cases where, to quote Cardinal Newman, *"Egotism is the true modesty."*

Where the expression of the Primary Word I-Thou is at least adequately present there is no place for the great heresies and nonsenses of the age, such as the assertion that economics is the bottom line; that the end of "Education, Education, Education", as it is grandly evoked, is to enable us to compete successfully in the modern (what else might it be, one asks oneself) world, and /or turn ourselves into the flexible work force that will adapt itself to the thrusting technological advances of the day.

I am myself for the most part a retired member of that modern world, the little paid work that I still do is in Counsellor Supervision, in other words I try to be as helpful as I can with the issues the counsellors who come to me raise, issues for example in connection with the cases they have and sometimes issues to do with colleagues, or the institutions they work for themselves.

Another justification I might claim for still having something to say on this matter is that I do retain quite a few connections with students and colleagues from the past and in the present. My retirement does not seem to shield me at all well from experiencing, if often at second hand, the ravages of this so-called modern world in terms, as I see it, of the relative absence in it of the understanding of the Primary Word I-Thou.

"Das Grundwort Ich-Du kann nur mit dem ganzen Wesen gesprochen werden."

The German 'Grundwort' is, I think, stronger than the common English translation 'Primary Word'; the at-the-bottom-of-all-things word I-Thou can only be spoken with the whole being, the at-the-bottom-of-all-things word I-It (or He or She) can never be spoken with the whole being. These are the two ways in which we encounter and are encountered. There is no need to get into a tangle of abstractions to try and explain what Buber means about these two fundamentally different, yet crucially compatible ways of meeting and being met. We know the difference.

Here's a lady who clearly doesn't expect to be met as Thou (as that which, as Buber puts it, for its moment fills the circle of Heaven). She expects to be met as an object, someone who at best may be remembered; oh yes, the lady whose husband died of cancer some weeks ago. She doesn't anticipate filling anyone's circle of heaven however briefly. Will she be remembered? So she gives her husband's name and ward number, and she'd better send an SAE, hadn't she. But she desperately needs to be met. Here she is writing to the Macmillan Hospital Support Nurse.

"Dear Jean,

> *sorry I dont know if it was Mrs or Miss. I hope you can remeber you give my Husband your Card in the Hospitall. I think it was the day before he came home it was the 21st of January. My Husband Died on the 22 Febuary a month after. why I'm writing to you is the Doctor told me he my Husband knew he had cancer since 1995. I just cant accept that he knew all that Time & never told me. he did tell me about you being to see him but he did not mention the word cancer as he knew the sister sent for me on the 20 Janary and told me but he did not want to talk about it. all I want from You is could you please tell me: what my Husband was like when you talked to him I know he must have guessed what it was as I had an Idea for the last 8 month but I realy thought there was hope. but from coming out of Hospital in January he went Rapid. I could not beileve it. he was a Great Husband & we had been married over 48 yrs. & I loved him & still do very mutch. I'm sorry we did not contact you in the month before he died. but he was so poorly he Just could not be bothered with any-one he Just wanted me & I never left him I have a Good Famly near me. the only thing is I'm deaf a bit & I've got a broken Heart. I dont want you to go out of your way if you Just write on a Sheet of Paper what he was like on the day you saw him and what he said Then I might get Peice of Mind.*

> Thanking You very mutch I am sending a Stamped Adress envelope.
>
> ***Mrs. B. Overton,***

> *My Husbands Name was George Overton I think it was Ward 1 he was in."*

She is encountered as Thou however. Not to be able to hear that through this reply would be to be deaf indeed.

"Dear Mrs. Overton,

Many thanks for your very moving letter. May I extend to you my very sincere sympathy at your sad loss, and say how touched I was by the things you wrote concerning your husband.

I would very much like to help you through this very sad time, and am very willing to help you seek answers for the questions you raised. However, rather than do this through a letter, I wonder whether you would be able to come to the hospital to see me, so that we could meet and talk face to face.

I will arrange transport to collect you and return you home safely, so if you are willing to come and see me, and I do hope you are able to, please contact my Secretary and she will arrange an appointment.

Once again, may I say how moved I was at your sadness, and I will do all I can to ease the pain you are going through. Take care.

Yours sincerely, **Jean**
Macmillan Hospital Support Nurse"

The outcome was a meeting, just the one, which seems to have been wholly sufficient to enable the lady to feel fully met and heard. Both the meeting and of course the letter that led to it gave her what she profoundly needed, the opportunity to give a local habitation and a name to that which had been so agonizing in the experience of her husband's illness and death, and in the subsequent weeks.

To be met as Thou. In January 1999 I underwent massive surgery for cancer of the oesophagus. I had to be operated on a second time two days later owing to the unexpected development of a large blood clot. In the time between the operations I had some experiences that have given me pause for thought. It was during the night before it became clear that another operation would be necessary that a negativity the like of which I have never known came upon me. In Intensive Care there is a nurse allocated to each patient all the time, and there is lots going on. Once when I awoke I remember seeing a blurred picture of what looked like a group of nurses talking. together. Somehow or other it was quite clear to me that they found me troublesome and unendurable. I imagined I heard something like, *"We don't like him"*. I haven't the slightest doubt this is not how things were, negativity makes its own form of imagined reality. It is, however, what I experienced, and I remember thinking I saw them turn their backs and move away from me all together, before I lapsed again into unconsciousness. When I came to a while later, again unutterably bereft and achingly lonely, I heard subdued but cheerful voices chatting away somewhere to my left. After a while I couldn't bear any longer not to call out from my well of loneliness. Someone came and said it was they who had the job of looking after me, which I interpreted in my negativity as meaning that it certainly wasn't a job they would have chosen. In answer to my expression, as I recall it, of utter loneliness and longing to be talked with, to be taken up in company, the memory is of being told to rest, to go to sleep, to-morrow I would have to be ready again to do the hard work, the breathing exercises to re-expand the deflated lung, and so on. In amongst all of this the comfort I remember finding was to say to myself that they weren't doing their job properly, and much as I didn't want to, and I certainly didn't, for my own and subsequent others' sakes, I would have to shop them next day, and tell the surgeon about their failure to hear the profound need of at least this one of their patients.

I have talked about this experience more than once. At first I told it as a kind of 'Hallucinations people have in hospital' tale - 'Strange Things that Happen in Intensive Care'- there would be some truth in that version of the story and I am fully aware how very well I was for the most part looked after. I now think though that it is more interesting than that, even if the events as I recall them were in fact, at least in part, hallucinatory. It is as if my need to be met as Thou, not just treated sensibly and well-managed - "oh, reason not the need", was overwhelming, and that I did not experience this as happening. Yet at the same time, thanks perhaps to a lifetime of many trusts met, and probably more importantly, to a childhood in which my need to be known truly as me, was very sufficiently met, I could put my not quite overwhelming need on hold. I would at some later time, I could tell myself, certainly be met and my grim experience would be recognised and taken on; as one might say the old lady's broken heart was entirely met, taken on and for its moment filled the circle of heaven for the Macmillan nurse. The latter, by the way, and many of her colleagues who did similar work, was under fairly routine contemporary management style attack at the time; called to sudden meetings, required to make presentations to justify their existence in the jobs they had been appointed, often long enough ago, by management itself to do and so on. *"For God's sake fight them off,"* I found myself saying. *"The fight isn't just for your sake, it's for all our sakes. Who will be there for us in extremis, at the end of our life, say; who will control the young doctors who might harry us into another pointless ordeal when our time has come? Who, when we are in need of it, will give us the truth and our loved ones the truth in an I-Thou encounter when the word is spoken with the whole being? Who will do that if such as you with your grasp of what the work truly is are to be swept away by the all-powerful requirements of that well known Bottom Line of Economics?"* Sure we know, unless we have got horribly lost, what an I-Thou meeting is, however brief a moment it may occupy, and whom or whatsoever it may be a meeting with. We know indeed the difference between the Primary Words I-Thou and I-It.

Nothing the matter with the I-It meeting and I-It relationships of course. That is after all the terrain in which for the most part we carry on our lives. After the old lady's letter and her broken heart have been wholly encountered and taken up the objectifying world comes quite properly into its own, files are looked up, diaries consulted, arrangements made. Fine. It is just the utter absence of the encountering and taking up and being taken up, that leads to shipwreck.

Ofsted stories are ten a penny. I'll be economical; here are extracts from a couple of letters from past PGCE students, extremely able people both and both in senior positions as heads of large departments.

> *"We suffered **OFSTED** last term- an extraordinary experience from which the English Dept. emerged smelling of Christian Dior and yours truly was patted on the head a great deal. My primary response was a mixture of exhaustion, relief and a little pride. Well, we had worked very hard to get things as the Inspectorate wished and so... what? Now it's all gone and the shit thickens. The publication of the report to parents, the press, the **ACTION PLAN** (Aaarghh! Action Plan, Targets, Value Added, Development Plan...) What has happened? Had I seen this coming I would have had done with it and just gone straight into plastic corrugated roofing or rivets or advertising."*

> *"And **OFSTED**, may the Lord preserve us. What an anguished, shameful torture that was. We had our visit last term. They were so intrusive I began to think I would find an inspector at home with me giving me a mark out of seven for how well I did my ironing or cleaned my teeth. I am dismayed that I find myself typing the following words: I was given a Chris Woodhead certificate for being A Really Good Teacher. Well, I can rest easy now. Curiously, I felt it to be a warm stroke for about ten minutes, but now it feels rather like having the camp guards tell you you're a model prisoner. Do you know the line in A Man For All Seasons when Thomas More tells Richard Rich to be a teacher? Rich says he can't bear the idea: he wants a place at court. He asks who will ever know he's good at what he's doing. More replies, 'You will know you're a good teacher. Your pupils will know. God will know. Not a bad audience that.' I cling to that. It's what's in your heart that matters."*

In any I-Thou encounter of course both parties are most wholly themselves. No encounter of that sort is indicated in either of these accounts, each writer feels unmet and ultimately unknown, objectified instead as a caricature or stereotype. One might argue of course that to imply a general state of affairs merely from two examples is statistically suspect. Maybe my own encounters with teachers, however, lead me to the conviction that the contemporary obsession with measurement, inspection and judgement (at the end of which lies the practice, well rehearsed incidentally in Nazi Germany, of Naming and Shaming) can have the most terrific effect and unbounded consequences. I-Thou encounters cannot be structured in by management systems; they cannot be contrived at all. There is always something of the miraculous in their appearance; but strenuous and successful efforts can certainly be made to structure them out. Can one detect anything other than institutional structuring out of the I-Thou encounter between Ofsted inspectors and teachers in the prose we hear in this reply from the Department of Education in response to a letter I wrote to the Minister of Education some time ago expressing my considerable anxiety about Ofsted and its consequences?

> *"**OFSTED's** Framework for Inspection provides a consistent criteria against which all schools are inspected. By its very nature, such a rigorous inspection is likely to cause some apprehension amongst those inspected and may be stressful for some staff. The Government believes that the educational benefits of inspection far outweigh any inconvenience which a school may face.*
>
> *The level of apprehension amongst some staff will lessen as inspections become a more accepted part of school life. It must also be remembered that inspectors go into schools to inspect the normal activities of the school. There should therefore be no great changes in working practices over the period of the inspection, nor should staff feel pressured into over-performing for the inspectors' benefit."*

I have read that to a few teachers. The gentlest response tends to be the old Mandy Rice Davies-ism 'Well, they would say that, wouldn't they.' Fear, humiliation, bravado, early retirements, nervous breakdowns, more fear. It's an old tale by now and anyone with honest connections with teaching could go on adding to it. But what is it that is most damaging about this tale of distorted and distorting encounters, this story of the doors barred against the I-Thou encounter? I would like to start my answer to that in the middle of an exceptionally good story, namely, Tolstoy's *War and Peace*. Prince Andrei Bolkonsky has fallen in love with the youngest daughter of Count Rostov and he is listening to her singing one evening in the Rostov family home.

"He looked at Natasha as she sang, and something new and blissful stirred in his soul. He felt happy and at the same time sad. He had absolutely nothing to weep about, yet he was ready to weep. For what? For his past love? For the little princess? For his lost illusions?... For his hopes for the future?... Yes and no. The chief reason for his wanting to weep was a sudden acute sense of the terrible contrast between something infinitely great and illimitable existing within him and the narrow, material something, which he, and even she, was. The contrast made his heart ache, and rejoiced him while she sang."

That paradox, in terms of the language used which lies at the heart of our existence, namely, those two absolute and incompatible knowledges - that which for ever hedges us in and limits us, 'the narrow, material something', which Kierkegaard calls our Necessity, and over against it that which utterly denies limitation, 'the infinitely great and illimitable', which Kierkegaard calls our Possibility (and for clarity's sake those are the terms, Necessity and Possibility, that I will stick to); a paradox, which is also implicit in the title of one of Newman's most striking sermons, *The Greatness and Littleness of Human Life*. There isn't much place for Possibility if your letter asserting a broken heart should chance to fall into the vortex of a hospital bureaucracy that has lost its apprehension that a patient can and for their moment must fill the circle of heaven; there isn't much place for Possibility when the Grim Reaper takes his seat at the back of the class and we 'poor, bare, forked animals' are up for judgement.

To deny the narrow, material something that one is, i.e. to deny one's Necessity, is, of course, nonsense and leads potentially to disaster; not to recognise or to lose contact with the infinitely great and illimitable existing within one, one's Possibility, is equally potentially disastrous. I do not know how it is for other people, for me, however, that apparently paradoxical character attaching to one's consciousness of one's life, that it is hedged in by Necessity and illimitable in its Possibility has been of the hugest significance throughout my life. Kierkegaard didn't I think so much teach me anything new about that, what he did do for me a few years ago was clarify it and give it form, name and habitation. It was on a holiday that I read his *Sickness Unto Death* (odd choice maybe, but so it was). It was a rather special holiday that we took for various reasons a few years ago, the sea journey round the coast of Norway from Bergen to the Russian frontier and back. A ship leaves Bergen every day to do the 11 day round trip, calling in at dozens of settlements, from great cities such as Trondheim, to tiny settlements in Fjords, shadowed by snow-capped peaks, delivering goods for local businesses and shops, picking things and people up, and dropping them off; a kind of bus and train service where there are no through roads or rail links. 'The Most Beautiful Journey in the World' it proclaims itself and not without justice. Cruising through the Lofoten Islands; harbouring in Molde in a great ring of distant snow-capped mountains; experiencing the wild, remote Trollfjord; walled in by perpendicular mountain sides; maybe most of all, sailing through the Arctic in bright sunshine in the early hours of the morning with the snow-covered cliffs of North Norway to the right and the North Pole some hundreds of miles to the left and nothing save small islands, sea and ice between. It was a splendid experience. But it certainly wasn't all that it might have been. Necessity hedged it in as it always does. It was bitterly cold for one thing and one cannot switch on one's sense of the illimitability of things just to suit the landscape. Happily, as often happens with something special, the experience of that journey seems to have grown fuller by means over which I have no conscious control, and my sense of Possibility has been added to in ways beyond those of my conscious making. An obvious enough truth, but one I had not grasped until I found it articulated for me by Rainer Maria Rilke: these days in their turn become transformed into a gift and a treasure.

Again, I cannot know how it is for others, but during the course of my life there have occurred particular moments which seem to have a very special significance. The one I treasure as representing for me the directest sense of boundless Possibility took place when I was about 18, standing with a friend outside the gates of the grandiose 18th century castle which the school had recently, and rather astonishingly, bought for the even then not all that princely sum of around £12,000. I am sure that I have invested significance in that memory since then to the degree that there isn't really a pure memory (whatever that might be) left. I don't think that matters, what I do have is what one might call a kind of constructed recollection of that moment when, on looking up from the village street to the boundless skies, I knew that there were no bounds. It was a kind of all shall be well and all manner of things shall be well knowledge. There have been other such moments and when I talk about experiences such as these I am sure that I am not talking about anything the slightest bit out of the way. I don't know how common they are, very I imagine, perhaps universal. But they are not the kind of thing people in our society talk about very much. To do so might be to incur similar risks as those incurred by people who admit to talking to the birds, and the plants and bushes in the garden. You can do that kind of thing if you are mediaeval and saintly, not if you are 20th century and rational. Which we all are, aren't we? It is a lot easier to let such moments wither away, rather as the plants may eventually do, unvalued and untended. To the rubbish dump with them! Economics is the bottom line. Facts are what count; and don't forget it.

When I was told by letter last October that the results of a relatively routine endoscopy, checking on an oesophagus condition that I had had for years, were not, unfortunately, normal this time, and would I please come into hospital to discuss the implications with a specialist in a few days, it was pretty clear to me that I had cancer. I'd always known that was a possibility. It wasn't an easy few days and one of the ways in which I handled it was to write to the specialist, telling him at some length how I wanted to be told whatever it was that he was going to have to tell me. I knew quite well what I was up to. I can to a fair degree hold on to the knowledge (I do not know what else to call it) of the infinitely great and illimitable existing in me, and I am wholly at one with Jung when, as it seems to me, he expresses fundamentally the same, and asserts that what gives meaning to life is to know that one is an actor in the divine drama and, "that everything else is banal and you can dismiss it. A career, the producing of children, all are maya compared with that one thing, that your life is meaningful." But I needed, naturally enough, to keep myself as well fortified as I could, especially if I might shortly be told, as seemed quite possible, not just that I was very much a narrow, material something, which I know perfectly well, but a doomed one into the bargain. As the German Jewish philologist Victor Klemperer, whose spirit (and body too) survived the Nazis largely thanks to a relentless study of what was happening to the German language during those terrible years, puts it, 'Words can be like tiny doses of arsenic, after a while follows their effect.' I didn't want to be lied to, but like the lady with the broken heart there was a variety of ways in which I could be addressed. I knew I could be told what might appear to be the whole truth in such a way (and that I might hear it in such a way) that I might in effect be poisoned and my sense of Possibility wiped out, my place in the divine drama eclipsed. The specialist's first comment at our meeting was to say that he had never before had a patient write quoting Wittgenstein at him. 'Worte sind Taten', 'Words are Acts', I had written, and they are, and to have leaned a little on that great 20th century exposer of the labyrinthine trickery of language was, I think, entirely reasonable on my part. The specialist still had to tell me I had cancer (operable as it turned out), and he did it very well and I heard him, so to speak, unencumbered, because I was as well equipped as I could make myself with Necessity, the ultimately, anyway, doomed organism, and with Possibility, the sense of the unboundedness of things; in other words with that paradox of the Greatness and Littleness of human life, which only seems like a paradox because of the limitations of language. It is a struggle though, one needs all the support one can get to hold in balance that apparent paradox, and it did me no harm at all, some two or three weeks later, to read this paragraph at the end of a letter from an old school friend (the one incidentally who had been standing outside the school's castle gates with me, nearly 50 years ago now), written in reply to my letter telling him about the diagnosis, 'so, after the initial shock, then the sadness, comes the very positive feeling your letter leaves me with. As we struggle to find the shape of the great plan, it finds us and shapes us. And in spite of everything it seems quite sane to believe (with Mother Julian of Norwich) that 'all shall be well'. In our heart of hearts, somehow and miraculously, we know this to be true.'

In my letter to the specialist I had, you might say, been protecting myself before the event; my two ex-students in their remarks about the Ofsted inspections they had been subjected to were in part at least themselves after it. They too, it seems to me, are by implication equally clear about the terrible threat to Possibility, to the great and illimitable in themselves, and, because in themselves, in the work they are doing too. Not everyone is so well equipped for self-defence. It is difficult to imagine the lady with the broken heart protecting herself with mockery or irony, or calling Wittgenstein to her side, if the voice of bureaucracy alone had responded to her need, however courteously and efficiently. Very few of us experience life in such a way that we can easily hold on to, let alone recognise and respond to our apprehension of the great and illimitable within ourselves. The narrow, material thing very easily takes centre stage, as it does in our observation of and work with other people.

It seems surprising to me now how relatively recently it occurred to me that those two great ideas of Buber and Kierkegaard, or rather their expression of them, which gave them such living form for me, are in effect two aspects of the same thing. When the Primary Word I-Thou is spoken Possibility is addressed. When the whole being encounters the Other the great and illimitable is in the encounter. Not so when the Primary Word I-It (or He or She) is spoken. Here Necessity, namely that whose limits are knowable, is being addressed, which is fine so far as it goes and which is indeed what mostly happens. Disastrous, however, if it is all that happens.

Let us try to give these abstractions living form again and take ourselves off to Sheffield some 25-30 years ago. A colleague from my early teaching days, and for many years now a good friend, had, in mid career, got a bit fed up with what he was doing. Teaching Sums he sometimes called it sardonically. During his 'A'level and degree days (he did a Mathematics degree) he didn't think a great deal about the job future. Nor, I must admit, did I. Get a good degree first, the word was, then you can think about how you are going to earn a living, first things first; and he went along with that more or less. We could afford to in those days; unemployment wasn't in prospect. So he ended up teaching Maths, and a dozen years later felt he would like to try a teaching job that might perhaps feel more, or at least differently, fulfilling. He took a year off to train for teaching children with special educational needs. It went well, and the first available job after training which was for a limited period, perhaps covering a pregnancy, was in a school for children with the spina bifida condition. That went well too and he was sorry when the job came to an end. Next he was asked to work in a school for spastics. (Whether one can still use that word in terms of being politically correct or not is something I come back to briefly a little later.) We used to meet up occasionally for a drink in those days. He was pretty miserable in the school and came to feel more and more that he couldn't really cope with the work. In the end he gave the new project up and went back to teaching Maths which he continued to do contentedly for many years, so the story has a happy enough ending. I tell it because it seems to me to illustrate very nicely the difference between being able to experience Possibility in what one meets, and thus be open to the chance of the I-Thou encounter, and on the other hand being able to experience Necessity only, nothing but the narrow and material thing, and thus be open merely to the I-It encounter. Given his life experience up to that time the spina bifida children with their unimpaired intellectual ability could easily enough be met as Thou, and as illimitable by my friend. Not so the spastics, and he knew to his credit that that wasn't at all how things should be, and that, if it was anybody's fault, it was his not theirs. That I think is roughly what he felt. I don't imagine either of us in those days would easily have found our way into a language which could have expressed the feelings; and that, in my view, is where the great value of voices such as those of Buber and Kierkegaard lies, they give direct and powerful form to truths that might otherwise lie forever inarticulate within us, become damaged, or atrophy through lack of use.

I taught infants on supply once for half a term. I had no training for it and was no good at it. I have been able to see since and could see then I think that I had little grasp of the Possibility in children of that age. I became a good deal less blind to it when I didn't have a class of 37 to cope with on my own, and when, retired by then from full time work, I helped out, mostly by listening to readers in my wife's infant class. Unthreatened I could begin to grow open to the possibility of the I-Thou encounter. As an example of the atrophy of this I recall the Primary Head who said à propos my enquiry about the children in her school who might be expected to be academic achievers in subsequent schools, 'We don't have that kind of child here.' The more you think about it, the more chilling such a statement is, human beings categorised and placed; being met exclusively through the Primary Word I-It, exclusively as the 'narrow, material thing', 'the poor, bare forked animal.'

One might think that the one thing needful for a teacher training course would be to secure a learning that enables people wholly to understand that things have gone badly wrong and that one must change them or get out, whenever a situation has developed or is encountered where the door has slammed shut on Possibility, where the I-Thou address has become unimaginable. This is bound to be so and of course whenever there is a bottom line, whether it be economics, or particular results or measurable and measured accountability. This, for example, from an H.M.I. report (my choice of it is fairly arbitrary, one does not have to search far for this kind of officialese). There are to be, we are told, 'enterprise audits which evaluate teaching and learning styles and annual school audits where senior staff spend one day reviewing all aspects of a school's work. Many institutions are working to sharpen their quality assurance procedures by systematising the use of performance indicators and peer review.'

Not a glimmer there that might let in a glint of I-Thou possibility. Foursquare we have it, the objectifying world of the Primary Word I-It; and bereft of its heavenly partner it falls hopelessly into crude and crass assumptions. Those scarcely definable, infinite subtleties, teaching and learning styles for example; they are to be evaluated, just like that, and by enterprise audits, no less. Of course it is senior staff who will do the annual review; after all promotion is bound to throw up the most competent and reliable, isn't it. As for peer review, where could any problem possibly lie, since we all respect and trust each other, don't we. Fear? Envy? Mutual hostility? Forget it. As for the language itself, it is so much that of the desiccated calculating machine that it immediately becomes self-satirising. This kind of language is dislocating and dishonest because to look at things with the accompanying possibility of the I-Thou meeting cut out of the equation is to look through a glass so darkly that one is unlikely to see anything beyond a distorted reflection.

Harm is bound to be inflicted by teaching which has lost touch with the I-Thou. When the apprehension of the learner's Possibility is not there, and he or she has become a nothing but; a spastic indeed. We would have had no need of a new term for spastic had that word not become a nothing but term. People enjoy being sarcastic about politically correct language, at best though it would not evolve unless we needed to find new forms of expression when Possibility has been lost to the old, and the mere lees of Necessity left.

Here now is a very different kind of voice, that of Rilke, again, writing early this century. He was captivated by a school he visited in Sweden. Looked at from our late twentieth century perspective it sounds to have been not untypical of a number of experiments in post Tolstoyan educational idealism, a sort of Scandinavian Summerhill perhaps. We might have our questions about it, but what seems to me not to be in doubt is the rightness of Rilke's passionate espousal of what one might call educational agnosticism. We do not know and never could know the real outcomes of education should we sharpen our quality assurance procedures to a razor's edge.

> *"The simple joyfulness of the place," he writes, "is rooted in the profoundest seriousness. The school isn't locked into any programme, it is open on every side. Training, knowing how to educate people isn't at all the matter in hand. This is not what the school is about. Who is it anyway that can be a trainer and educator of others; who among us may assert that right?*

> *What the school attempts is simply this - to disturb nothing. While it does its work with vigour and devotion however, while it eases from their path whatever may stand in people's way, while it raises questions, truly listens, observes, teaches and wisely loves, it does everything that may be done by adults for those who are to follow after them."*

And a little further on in his account,

> *"One has the conviction that this is a place in which a person can truly become something. This school is not some preliminary to real life, life is on its way here. The school may have adopted a smaller scale so that it can be encompassed by those who are not yet fully grown; yet life is here in full possibility."*

And that's about it really, the difference between those completely contradictory ways of thinking about and making connections between one another; on the one hand the H.M.I. document and my reply from the Department of Education for example, on the other voices such as those of Rilke and the Macmillan nurse. The latter are suffused with a sense of Possibility, wholly open to the ordinary miracle of the I-Thou encounter, the former embedded in a false knowledge of outcomes and the consequences of these, bent on the systematisation and judgement of them, cabin'd, cribb'd, confined by Necessity, held irrevocably in the objectifying world of I-It. The lady with the broken heart, the teachers at the receiving end of the Ofsted inspections, me waiting to find out if I have cancer and be told what that will mean, all of us, so to speak, spastics in the world. It isn't just that we need to be addressed as Thou and thus to remain, in human terms, indefinable; the really important thing is that if we are not so addressed, if it is not understood that we should be so addressed, we are going to be completely missed and turned into the absurd images of a distorting mirror, and how, trapped in the place of distorting mirrors can we ever know, or have any faith in the knowledge that somehow, inexplicably, all shall be well.

Now I am very suspicious of an ending with that kind of rhetorical flourish, even when I've written it myself. I think what I have learned from this is that I need to search out if I can why it is that I feel about these things as I do. I need to explore why it is that living with, indeed in, agnosticism, in the sense of living in uncertainty; truly accepting that one can only look through a glass darkly; doing without, in Keats' phrase, an 'irritable reaching after fact and reason', seems to me not at all unfortunate and restricting but rather a wonderfully positive state of affairs.

Faith

I want to begin this section by suggesting that there is often a deep and crucial difference between having beliefs about things and, on the other hand, having faith in things. Holding and indeed proclaiming beliefs about people, institutions, ideas, or whatever else turns so easily into the dogmatism of certain knowledge and thus into limitation, the claustrophobia of Necessity, while having faith in them, insofar as it is truly faith, implies the wealth and boundlessness of Possibility.

It often seems these days as if we can only confer value or deny it to people, or institutions, or ideas if we can measure them up and down, and round and about, and put quality control labels on them. A school or hospital, say, having been quantified and quality controlled may find itself starkly designated as Failing, or at the other end of the scale the label may read "Centre of Excellence". If things really go its way it might even find itself sailing serenely into the future as a Flagship. And the labels and statistics attached are printed out for all to see and know, and acquiesce to, and for the most part we do so acquiesce. We do confer on the results and the accompanying facts and figures that kind of belief which claims for itself the status of certain knowledge, the kind not open to question.

Some while back the Physics Department of a nearby University was given 24 out of 24 after its inspection. Unto whom can be granted more than everything? A Flagship indeed, and not an iceberg to be seen. Yet do we not need to grasp that in the end belief of this kind, drawing as it does its power from the categorical certainty with which it expresses itself, turns out to be a miserably poverty stricken thing, and at worst a horribly distorting and damaging one, in comparison with the so much richer and essentially agnostic phenomenon which in what follows I am calling faith in things.

> *"Most of a working lifetime in teaching, a whole career - to be marked by Ofsted out of 7 next week."* This from a teacher friend of many years, one of those with that indispensable quality of the teacher, the capacity, to purloin Martin Buber's words, *"to be really there, to be and remain truly present to the child,"* and to have *"gathered the child's presence into her own store as one of the bearers of her communion with the world."*

Actually she had got it wrong, it wasn't done like that, a categorical judgment was not, apparently, being made. Mind you, a "profile of the quality of (her) teaching" as it was called which was intended "to assist in the management of the school" could hardly be experienced as anything other than a judgment passed upon her lifetime's work, and on the face of it "Satisfactory or Good" doesn't sound that depressing. The three categories were that one, and on either side of it Excellent or Very Good, and Less than Satisfactory. Why is it though that this kind of thing so knocks the stuffing out of people? Why, after subjection to the treatment, does it cost people, and many testify to this, such an effort to pull themselves back up and feel fully engaged in their work again? Largely, I suppose, because they feel so unknown and unrecognised, so completely objectified, so wholly It.

The members of staff apparently went a little wild when the Head Teacher suggested disclosing the categories they had all received to the heads of departments. One hopes that even the Excellent or Very Goods would have gone at least mildly wild at such a prospect. "Pinned and wriggling on the wall" indeed, "this is you, Satisfactory or Good, round about 4 or 5 out of 7 say".

I wonder in which category one of the most memorable of my own past school teachers would have found himself if he had been subjected to that treatment, if the Grim Reapers or, more accurately perhaps, the Day of Judgement men had observed along with a handful of others what to me was one of his most memorable lessons. Distinctly Less than Satisfactory most probably. He didn't do anything right, he came in, read to us and went out; no attempt to explain the literary genre; no tasks set; no follow up; no evident learning at all; and no visible lesson plan. Come to think of it he did get one thing right, the timing, the bell went just as he finished. It was Matthew Arnold's *Sohrab and Rustum*,

> *"And the first gray of morning filled the east,*
> *And the fog rose out of the Oxus stream."*

And the terrible, majestic story rolls on until as night falls,

> *...."the new bath'd stars*
> *Emerge and shine upon the Aral Sea."*

You don't have to like that kind of thing, but you might, who knows, it might even become a lifetime's treasure.

He certainly wouldn't have got any credit in his profile for a moment such as the one where he passed me, a 15 year old, in the school yard and said, as I remember it, *"It's time you read The Mayor of Casterbridge"*. Nor would my teacher friend with the middling profile, for all those infinitely varied moments of true meetings on corridors or wherever when she encounters a child exactly as he/she needs to be encountered, and might even to his/her infinite joy do her impeccable impression of Cartman in TV's *South Park*, *"You're being totally immature"*, *"Do it again miss, please!"* As Cardinal Newman has it (talking of

Universities but it might just as well be schools), *"a [school] is an Alma Mater ... knowing her children one by one, not a foundry or a mint or a treadmill,"* and nor, I'd be inclined to add, a Sink school or a Flagship.

Ever since his part in those liberating, life-enhancing sketches in the late '50s show *Beyond the Fringe*, I have admired and been indebted to Jonathan Miller. In and amongst an extraordinary variety of activities, he is a wonderful director of operas. Despite its great reputation, I could never make much of Mozart's *Cosi fan tutte*; it seemed a cheap and silly story, quite unequal to the strain of bearing such sublimely beautiful music. Yet, while a Jonathan Miller production of the opera was not the only one to help me learn to make sense of the piece, it contributed very substantially to the process. Once again, I had cause to be grateful to him. It is the story of a couple of young men in love, and both of them equally in love with the idea of being in love; and of two young women in like case. An older friend of the two young men, a man of the world, seen it all before type, hears the two utter their protestations with a mixture of amusement, irritation and cynicism, and naturally their assertions of certainty in, and absolute belief about, their undying, eternal, equally reciprocated love grow ever more clamorous. The deep, delicate and rich phenomenon I want to call faith in things, which may have been beginning to develop between the respective couples is about to be put at risk of profound damage by the events as they unfold. The man of the world initiates a plan that will put their assertions of absolute belief to the test. The young men will pretend to their lovers that they are called to the wars, and will return in disguise to try their luck wooing the other's girl. Not that there could be any such luck of course, no chance! And there for a moment we will leave them.

Round about the time when what seemed like the entirely satisfying irreverence of *Beyond the Fringe* was giving me such delight, another encounter came my way that has proved equally liberating and long lasting, and that was seeing Carol Gustav Jung interviewed on TV by John Freeman in the then celebrated *Face to Face* series. I was 23, and by then I didn't have a lot of belief left, not of the confident sort that enabled me to feel I had the truth of things anyway. I remember late night conversations from those days, running the range from despair and disillusion to wild elation and helpless laughter, and one thing I remember very specifically, and that was my claim to have lost my belief in everything except the absolute wrong of capital punishment. It was still on the statute books in those days, indeed I had seen the black cap put on and sentence delivered a year or so earlier myself.

It was as though I was clinging on to that in order to retain at least one certain belief in which to ground myself, a kind of fertilizer out of which other beliefs might one day sprout. I lost that one too somewhere along the journey. I can't remember how long ago, it just slipped away. Not that I wouldn't vote against its reintroduction if I had to vote on the matter, but I don't hold a belief about the intrinsic wrong of it. Indeed belief, whenever I encounter assertions of it, seems to grow ever thinner, more pallid and off the track to me. An extraordinary moment it was when Freeman put the question to Jung, *"Do you now believe in God?"* I don't imagine I was the only person spellbound. *"Now?"* asked Jung, and there was a great long pause while the old man took his pipe out of his mouth and contemplated it. The world stood still. Then he quietly went on, *"Difficult to answer. I know. I don't need to believe. I know."* Why was that such a vivid moment? Why did I vow to myself, I'll get to know that chap some day? And I did get to know him very well many years later, when I had got over the conviction that the really famous names are unapproachably difficult and had realised, rather late in the day, that they are usually far more accessible and incomparably more interesting than their interpreters. He became and remains a very good companion whom I don't need to believe, but in whom I am very content to have faith.

The fairly low church Anglican belief system I had been brought up in had lost whatever significance it had had for me by then. I imagine I had already sensed that faith might be something quite other than belief in the form of dogmatic knowledge, and that the way towards it might have little if anything to do with belief of that kind. *"I don't need to believe,"* said the old man with his twinkling eye and his pipe, and I thought to myself , *"there is something infinitely valuable for me here"*. I think it was so valuable because it was the first time I had witnessed and grasped that crucial differentiation between the requirement that one should 'believe' and the actuality that one might at times know, and accept as central to life, a kind of 'faith in' which says in effect, "nevertheless, there is meaning"; of which more later.

We have left the two young men in *Cosi fan tutte* waiting long enough; each now in his disguise and engaged in wooing the other's supposedly eternally faithful beloved. If you don't already know the story, it all comes out just as you probably expected. Unimpeachable trustworthiness doesn't quite manage to hold out. The sublime music rolls on, and the human beings don't behave as well as they would like to have believed they would. Miller's way of bringing the story to its close is certainly not the only possible one, but it did prove to be a moving, yet disturbing and to many who saw it, profoundly appropriate alternative to the more usual ending with the couples appearing fully reconciled and ecstatically happy again. After all the trickery has been revealed, the deceptions laid open, and those categorically asserted beliefs about eternal love and trustworthiness that can never fail lie in ruins, a kind of dread falls upon everyone. The words of reconciliation are sung to the heart-easing harmonies, but nobody is convinced; damage, maybe irreparable, has been inflicted on the delicate strands of faith in each other that had been beginning to grow and develop between the couples. Still singing the lovely strains, they start to drift slowly apart from one another, and each leaves the stage by a different exit, slowly, hesitantly, casting behind uncertain looks.

What would it mean really to have faith in someone? I asked that question of a young man not so long ago. To some degree all of us are inevitably on the receiving end of the kind of double message of which the young man, as it seemed to me, had received a substantial dose, the message that says, " my faith in you is infinite, but if you don't fulfil this or that tacit, or indeed overt, expectation then I'm afraid you may well find that you have forfeited it". His answer was predictable enough. Yes, he could imagine being a parent or a teacher and having infinite faith in child or pupil. Eventually though, if the trust was constantly breached, so far as he could see, he would be bound to lose faith in child or pupil. How could it be otherwise, how can faith in something extend beyond the conditions for it? Isn't the idea of unconditionality a sort of nonsense and wasn't the question itself a trap, not wholly different from that of the man of the world in the opera?

In his celebrated *Tractatus*, Ludwig Wittgenstein announces in the Preface that his aim is

> ...."to draw a limit to thought, or rather - not to thought but to the
> expression of thoughts: what can be said at all can be said clearly,
> and what we cannot talk about we must pass over in silence."

He repeats that categorical remark as the very last line in the book. Yet, just before that conclusion come these unexpected and extremely pregnant remarks,

> "My propositions serve as elucidations in the following way: anyone
> who understands me eventually recognises them as nonsensical,
> when he has used them - as steps - to climb beyond them.
> (He must so to speak, throw away the ladder after he has climbed up it.)
> He must transcend these propositions, and then he will see
> the world aright."

Later on when Wittgenstein was having a great struggle to find anyone who would risk publishing the *Tractatus*, he wrote this in a letter to a publisher he thought might understand him and be interested; not surprisingly, it didn't have the desired effect; "I want to write that my book consists of two parts: of the one which is here, and of everything I have **not** written. And precisely this second part is the important one."

Many of those at the receiving end of the Schools Inspectors' profiles and assessments, who may well feel they have spent the better part of a rich and varied working lifetime in the business, might also take the view that what is missing from this disconcerting Day of Judgment performance is precisely that "important part". I remember very vividly a particular Board of Studies meeting when inspection was in the offing and closing fast, and this was in the days when such things were very much more benign, and the judgment more tentative, less categorical and less likely to lead to dramatic outcomes. It was fascinating and well worth pondering upon, to see the sudden attempts to clothe the chief inspectors, when their names were given, with familiarity and humanity. I remember the Science inspecting team's head, a Mr. Greene, turning suddenly into Vic - Vic Greene, you remember Vic. A colleague and I thought we'd better do something about the chief English examiner, a highly reputed figure in the trade called Mr. Arnold, so we christened him Tubby, Tubby Arnold. Naturally, he turned out to be tall and slim and distinguished looking. I suppose we thought we were just having some fun at the expense of all the silly stuff going on, but I am sure that we too were to a degree into the humanity bestowing business.

To Vic a Greene or to Tubby an Arnold, so to speak, is not however merely a superstitious and slightly desperate attempt to tame the potentially dangerous beast, one may well be indicating the wish to be met as a Thou and not merely an It, and a determination to be ready in oneself for such an encounter. It may reflect an implicit recognition that there must be in the transaction a second part, the important one, the part where judgments that demand belief have no place, where what is said is said by an I encountering a Thou.

To find oneself teaching in a comprehensive school that came quite close in the national statistics to having the worst public examination results in the country doesn't sound a very attractive prospect. Interesting therefore to encounter a staff member of such a school in recent times and find that being a teacher there had been for him a far richer and more worthwhile experience than working in any of his previous schools had been, in a career which had run nearly half its course and had included substantial spells of time in several schools. The reasons were not far to seek, not unexpectedly they were mostly to do with the quality of leadership and the measure of honesty and reality in the place. One thing only he was afraid of, people coming in from the outside and saying, "this is no good; none of it is any good; you're no good" - a judgement, namely, which asserts a belief and requires an assent, but which has nothing to say to the teacher for whom the second, the important part, is no fantasy, but the most present reality; the teacher who knows what it means to have gathered the child's presence into his or her own store. Such a judgment has no connection with his or her faith in themselves; and the faith which develops between them and those amongst whom they work when things go right. Such judgments, disconnected from the delicate phenomenon of faith, are much more likely to do harm than good, as the assertions of belief, egged on by the man of the world, the sensible chap with his eyes wide open, did harm to the faith developing between the lovers in Mozart's opera. No wonder the first warm stroke of being "given a Chris Woodhead certificate for being a Really Good Teacher" lasted "for about 10 minutes", and then came to feel "rather like having the camp guards tell you you're a model prisoner". The second part wasn't there, or if at all thanks only to sheer good luck, the ladder hasn't been thrown away, the propositions haven't been seen as nonsensical and transcended, and the world is not being seen aright.

The following could, I suppose, be construed as some kind of an attempt to see the world aright, a wholly misguided one though, and one which shows no knowledge at all of the ladder which must be thrown away. It comes in the form of a questionnaire prepared by a university counselling service. Instant feedback has been all the rage for many a year, not even a half day's course worth its salt but doesn't hand out its form requiring to know instantly which bits of the morning's events were a Hit and which a Miss. How could counselling services dare remain behind the game and fail to hand over their questionnaire? This is how question 3 goes, "How effective was the treatment you received? Very, Somewhat, Adequate, Not Very, Not At All. Which aspects were Helpful, which Unhelpful?"

Here now a student who came for counselling a few years ago before such questionnaires came into fashion. She had been encouraged to come by a college official who discovered that she had had an impressive go at wrecking her room, and by others, including a doctor, who had seen the cuts she had inflicted on herself, especially her wrists. She was very unhappy and very hopeless; nobody really loved her or ever would, however much she loved them and however much she did for them. She was fat, ugly and not very clever, and unless she could be useful to them, no one had any time for her. I saw her on a dozen or so occasions over 2 or 3 terms, a period which included the long summer break. Goodness knows how she would have answered question 3, she'd never thought counselling would do any good, indeed she never believed that it had, although, as the letters reveal, something had. She might have ticked the "Not At All" box and I would have been open to judgment as a Really Bad Counsellor. On the other hand, she might have ticked "Very" or "Somewhat" in order to be nice to me. Personally, if I had had to fill the thing in as the counsellor, I'd have unashamedly ticked "Very" and would have had no trouble at all in detailing which aspects were Helpful. But that too would have been just as silly. I simply didn't and don't have, and nor should I, the kind of beliefs about the matter which can be expressed like that. Wittgenstein may have a point when he says, "what we cannot speak about we must pass over in silence", yet he does speak of that chance to see the world aright if we recognise the nonsensical; which I would certainly take to include holding the belief that all possibility must lie within and be encompassed by what we can speak about. A striking later remark of Wittgenstein's, *"if a lion could speak we would not understand him"*, seems to me to go nicely alongside Hamlet's famous reproof, *"there are more things in heaven and earth, Horatio, than are dreamt of in your philosophy"*. It does indeed seem as if it is possible sometimes to see the world aright. I still think I was doing so that day standing outside the gates of my old school, and there do seem to be ways that can be found to say something about that second part, the important one.

This is what the student wrote minutes after she had decided, to the surprise of both of us in the middle of a session, to finish with counselling and to say goodbye to it and to me. (Had there been an inspector disguised as a fly on the wall I would probably have been given 0 out of 4 for Endings Skills - this counsellor needs to develop and execute a more satisfactory Pathway to Endings; more about Pathways later on, this footprint will suffice for the moment.) So - the letter:

"Dear Rob,

> *It's 10 to 12 and I've just left you after saying goodbye. I'm glad I've got a few minutes to write and tell you how I feel right now. When I came to see you this morning I had no intention of ending our sessions, but I did feel differently about them. As I walked up here I felt really weird. Half of me felt, and still does feel, as though I've just made the biggest mistake of my life and I'm scared I can't cope without you. I came very close to turning round and making an appointment with you for next week. The other half of me feels as though I've finally begun to sort my life out ... I think maybe the counselling wasn't helping and that for once in my life I've decided to stop doing something even though I don't really want to."*

She concludes

"I know I always said that I didn't really think you could help me, but I know you have and you've changed me for the better. Even though I'm still a wreck and I have very little confidence, I feel as though you have given me some pride and self-esteem back, that I lost last February. I can remember all the nice things you've said about me. and that gives me a warm glow. I just wanted to make sure you know that, despite all my misgivings, I really do think you did a lot for me, and have helped me get through a difficult patch of my life. I'm really going to miss you so keep in touch."

I replied as well as I could. I was very happy about what she'd done and felt it was both brave and right. A couple of months later a final letter came, which I replied to, and I never heard anything more after that, which was fine by me. That's many years ago now, I hope her life is full and rich. I can't see any reason why it should not be. Here's part of that final letter:

.... *"the funny thing is I've never felt better. I feel so NORMAL, it's great .... Basically I'm trying to tell you I'm **really** happy.... I react in the way I genuinely feel and I feel like most people are really getting to know ME, as I really am. This can't be a bad thing as I haven't lost any friends! On the contrary I feel closer to people and they keep saying how happy I seem"*, and then after a thank you where she says, *"I always thought of you as a friend not a counsellor"* (more bad marks from the fly on the wall - needs to firm up his Boundaries Skills) and *"you always seemed to know just what to say to make me feel really special"*, she concludes, *"P.S. I'm drinking again, but only occasionally and this time for the right reasons!!!"*

What a nonsense to have passed over the questionnaire as she got up to leave during the last session. - Fill this in please, and state your beliefs, about yourself and me, and what's been achieved and how well. The second part, the important one? Rubbish. Everything must be judged and the consequent beliefs must be asserted and held. Faith? Faith developing between us that becomes unconditional and indestructible? What's that? You can't say anything clear or practical about that. You can't measure it, give it something out of 7 or 10, or profile it. It was there though, the words, as well as our experience, bear testimony to that. And there is absolutely nothing exceptional or remarkable about it. Such faith is the most ordinary thing. But its security is certainly not guaranteed. It can be badly hacked about. Questionnaires, Inspections, Targets to be Met or Else, Naming and Shaming, Profiles, Pathways and whatever else is in fashion; all that apparatus, insofar as it lays claim to being exclusive purveyor of the essential truths about people and institutions, and shows neither knowledge nor understanding of the second, the important part contributes mightily to the hacking about job, despite all the decent and sensible resistance people do try to put up against it.

"Yes", said the young man, "I would have faith in my children or my pupils, but it is possible that they could carry on in such a way that they would forfeit it." How, indeed, can I myself assert that nothing could have led me to lose faith in that student who came for counselling? She might have pulled a gun on me, as another student once did, a replica actually, but convincing enough to get him arrested when he did it too publicly. Yet that all seems beside the point, a separate issue; as if a quite different conception of faith has slipped in by the back door, a conception much more akin to the sort of belief that implicitly lays claim to being the purveyor of truths about people. And here a little story from Martin Buber, "no more", as he says,

> "... than this. I had a visit from an unknown young man, without being there in spirit. I certainly did not fail to let the meeting be friendly, I did not treat him any more remissly than all his contemporaries who were in the habit of seeking me out about this time of day as an oracle that is ready to listen to reason. I conversed attentively and openly with him - only I omitted to guess the questions which he did not put. Later, not long after, I learned from one of his friends - he himself was no longer alive - the essential content of these questions; I learned that he had come to me not casually, but borne by destiny, not for a chat but for a decision. He had come to me, he had come in this hour." He concludes thus, "What do we expect when we are in despair and go to a man? Surely a presence by means of which we are told that nevertheless there is meaning."

Only our own experience as givers and receivers of such presence (and sometimes too hearing or reading stories about such encounters) teaches us the difference between merely being there and being really there. One might however dare a kind of definition, namely that to have *"faith in"* is in truth that very being there, that very presence that Buber speaks of. It is precisely that gathering of the other into one's own store as one of the bearers of one's communion with the world, one of the focuses of one's responsibility for the world.

Put like that of course it sounds frightfully exalted and grand. It might be if it wasn't so ordinary and so all around us, happening any place and any time. Mostly we know when others are really there and when they are not, and we know, provided we have not got lost, when we are really there ourselves and when we aren't. There need be nothing self-evidently exalted or grand about this kind of faith. A little personal memory here, of one of the nurses who cared for me in hospital during the time I was there for my cancer operation. Seriously thinking of giving it all up she told me; so much paperwork now; lots of it to do with covering your back (wise, of course, one might have said to her in an age so enthusiastic to name and shame, and to solve all human problems by further adjustments of the management screw); no time now anyway as she sees it for what really matters, sitting on beds and talking to patients, her way, at least in part, of saying, being really there; her way of expressing that faith.

It certainly wouldn't have been difficult filling in a questionnaire just before I was wheeled out of hospital, but where could I have expressed anything about the reciprocal faith that I did experience? Not a faith that the operation would be certain to succeed, or some silly expression of faith in my wonderful courage and resilience that would be bound to carry me through. The sort of thing I'm talking of was all around me, just as its absence occasionally was. (Possibly those experiences I have written about of desolate times in the night in Intensive Care do in truth say something about moments of its absence.) I can perhaps best illustrate the positive experience by recalling the early appearances pretty well every morning of the surgeon (nothing to do with rounds), when he put his head round the door or came in briefly and asked the odd question and talked for a minute or two, telling me what Ordeals (my word - I found the mediaeval concept helpful) this day would hold for me. I knew myself to be in the presence of that kind of faith that had gathered me into its store, and that that would be how it was whatever might happen.

What a difference being within the purlieu of that kind of responsibility towards oneself from being looked after by those whose practice has become dominated by the requirement to get it right or else, be the *"or else"* humiliation by league table, naming and shaming, or whatever. How extraordinary to fall into the belief that the one thing needful is to set more targets, tighten the management screw, hone the quality assurance procedures, reward the good boys and girls, and punish the naughty ones.

The trouble with the kind of belief I have been writing about is that it is so seductive, and so easily draws those caught in its toils further into the trap of a kind of fundamentalism. A while ago the Macmillan nurse who wrote to the lady with the broken heart told me about a meeting with colleagues in the hospital. *"Pathways"* had become all the rage, maybe they still are. On the agenda was an item calling for the working out and institution of one such Pathway, in effect a Pathway to Death; a system, that is, for handling the last 48 hours of a person's life; planning the items not to be missed and the appropriate actions to be taken; not unlike an airline pilot going through all the complex and essential routines before taking off into the blue yonder, only those executing this Pathway, so to speak, wouldn't of course be going on the trip themselves.

In one of his books, Jung suggests that if you are going to be working seriously with people and taking a full part in your encounter with them, you must study and read and learn everything you are able to in order to prepare yourself as fully as you conceivably can, and then you must put all that to the back of your mind and go to the meeting in what is by implication a sort of agnostic faith, trusting that what needs to be called forth will be, whatever the surprises and even shocks that may lie in the meeting. It sounds like an admirable plan. Few of us, however, are immune to the lure of a nicely weeded Pathway. Not that in this case it took long for at least some of those present to react to that agenda item with the contempt it deserved, prominent among them the Macmillan nurse who told me about that seductive Pathway to Death.

I was lucky to have the chance to act as supervisor (a harmless term if not taken at face value) with such a person for a few years. Much of her work was specifically to do with caring for people, and for their loved ones when necessary, while they were dying, mostly of cancer. Nothing has moved me and impressed me more than the way I experienced this work being done; much in it of the practical kind of course; pain control naturally, but so much more; such an easiness with and presence for the unexpected; for the dignity and nobility sometimes of the dying; for the naturalness and apparent readiness too; but above all so peremptory a sense of the absolute value and importance of the time, whatever duration it may have, during which a person is dying, not one based on any faith that carries a name, yet a most deep faith for all that; an acceptance, without any irritable reaching after fact or definition, of the presence of meaning, and thus itself a presence which testifies that *"nevertheless there is meaning"*. When I come to die may it be among people who are truly present, and who therefore do testify through their contact with me and my loved ones that "nevertheless there is meaning".

It isn't an idle hope to have; we encounter such presence and can provide such presence ourselves often enough in the ordinary run of life, provided faith has not been squashed clean out of us. The lady with the broken heart encountered it, so I think did the student with the damaged wrists who came to counselling; so too do the patients and the guests lots of the time at the hands of the staff and the carers of the hospital and the hospice; and reciprocally of course, it isn't a one way thing. My teacher friend, profiled with crippling flimsiness as Satisfactory or Good, and those other two teachers, reeling from the Ofsted experience, provide such presence richly in their work. So do lots of teachers, nurses, doctors and all variety of people (I only write of the worlds I know something about). But providing such presence can feel desperately against the odds when one is deluged by targets, initiatives, statistics, judgements, demands for accountability, and for the appearance of accountability. It is hard indeed to keep faith in the face of inflexible belief systems which abandon contact with everything save the objectifiable and the measurable; down which road lies waiting the Naming and Shaming of the Jews and beyond that, the more dreadful still.

One's prayer for the teachers, nurses, doctors and counsellors, and those carers too in the hospices on whose shoulders, so far at least, the hand hasn't yet fallen; one's prayer for all of us really is that we never end up completely seduced by dogmatic belief systems which ordain what is to be done and how, to the exclusion of all else, and do it with such pressure that we completely lose hold of our faith in the "great and illimitable existing within us", and become blind to the meaning which we can testify to through our contacts with each other. To say with my old school friend, "In spite of everything it seems quite sane to believe with Mother Julian of Norwich that all shall be well," becomes nonsense only when the nonsensical is not recognised, the ladder is not thrown away and there comes to be no possibility of seeing the world aright.

No Man's Land: Robert Graham

During my final years as a lecturer involved in teacher training and as a supervisor of counsellors I found myself growing increasingly upset about what was going on around me, especially in the areas with which I was most familiar, namely education and counselling. In addition to that of course I was, and continue to be on the receiving end of phenomena such as the Health Service, the media and so forth. Was it because I was growing old and past it that I was coming to feel so angry and powerless? That's the sort of thing that is supposed to happen to older people. They lose their marbles as the saying goes. Only it didn't seem to be just that, I didn't feel, and still don't feel, at all isolated in my anger, distress or sense of impotence, it didn't seem to be a function of age or position. The snag was, though, that so much that was going on seemed irreproachably sensible, and even overdue. Surely there was some need for regulation of the curriculum in schools, and how can one possibly argue against systems being installed to check that children really are learning what they are supposed to be learning, or against systems installed to determine that teachers are doing a decent job? As for counselling, clearly there is nothing the matter with volunteers provided they are carefully selected, properly trained and can be removed if they are doing more harm than good. It must be right though, must it not, to try to get more regulation into the system; to establish ways for judging the effectiveness of the work; to institute formal qualifications; to set up supervisory organisations of which all practitioners will eventually have to become members and to which they will have to be accountable? In similar vein how can one argue against the institution of more stringent means of increasing the accountability of medical practice, in hospitals, surgeries and so on, or indeed any kind of practice that has to do with working with people? Counter arguments can easily be, and are, shot dead as they raise their heads above the parapet. The installation, regulation and strengthening of accountability has to be right. Those with responsibility must see to it, so far as they can, that there remain no loopholes in the wire.

In what follows, however, and in the light of the ideas developed in the previous two sections I will suggest that, for all their self-evident attractions, the institution and practice of accountability and judgment making, and the closing of loopholes must, unless we are to do serious damage to each other, yield absolute supremacy to what for the time being I will call living and working as best one can in that most problematic, yet potentially most rich of places, No Man's Land.

Most of us have heard something about what happened on the first Christmas Day of the First World War, by which time stalemate had already been reached and the respective defensive lines stretched from the English Channel to the borders of Switzerland and had already assumed the positions they were to keep, with only marginal variation, for the next four years. The events that took place in the trenches on that day in 1914 have taken on an almost mythic quality, and no wonder – friendly meetings between the lines of undefended, vulnerable men during that most murderous of attritional conflicts. Over the parapets there appeared signals and countersignals, ceasefires were agreed, men peered over the top, took the risk and emerged unarmed into the No Man's Land between the trenches. Songs were sung, gifts exchanged, photographs of families back home offered and admired, even makeshift footballs kicked about. Then as night fell they all slipped back into their trenches. And it never happened again. The loopholes were closed, decisively and for good, platoon and company commanders made accountable by those in higher command to see to it that there was no further possibility of fraternisation, never again a hint of an I-Thou meeting between the Tommy and the Hun. The enemy must be and must remain an object merely, never a one of them that being met might, as Buber has it, for his moment fill the universe of the other. No Man's Land must never again be a place where faith in and between people might start to take shape. Belief in precisely who the enemy was, what he was like and what must be his fate resumed its grip, and, for the duration, No Man's Land was never again to be a place of Possibility, but was to remain the place of hopeless Necessity, where men met only to kill and die, to drown in shell holes and bleed to death on the wire.

From great things to very small ones. Here is a thank you letter from the health service trust to the Macmillan nurse who has featured previously in these pages, shortly before she left to take up another appointment. It comes from the Human Resources Department and is signed by a secretary not known to the recipient. It goes as follows:

"Dear Mrs -

> *I acknowledge receipt of your resignation letter dated 29 September 1999 and note that your last day of employment with the Trust will be 31 October 1999.*

> *May I take this opportunity to thank you on behalf of .... Health Care NHS Trust for your loyal and dedicated service over the last 6 years. Mr .... especially wanted to say a big thank you for all your valued working contributions to the .... Directorate. You will be missed by colleagues and friends.*

> *With best wishes for the future.*

> *Yours sincerely*   Miss .... Human Resources Department"*

It seems to have been something of a straw that broke the camel's back. The recipient writes this to the Mr .... referred to in the letter. He is manager of the Directorate within which the recipient's work for the Trust has been done:

"Dear Jim

> On the 29th September, I wrote to you giving notice from my present post. Today is my last working day at ...., and I have yet to receive from you any acknowledgement at all of my letter, or its contents.

> I have received a letter from Human Resources, which I can only describe as a dismal example of bureaucratic hoop-jumping and box-ticking.

> It refers to me as Mrs .... - a title I have never used in my clinical role; thanks me for the past 6 years - I have been here for 7 - and informs me that Mr .... specially wanted to thank me .... etc.

> Is it really not possible for 'Mr ....' to make some personal contact? Do you and 'Human Resources' really believe this level of communication is acceptable?

> I am aware that of the many complaints made against the Trust, a significant number have poor or inadequate communication as a component. From experience, I am not surprised. Somewhere along the line, we are losing our ability to 'meet' as fellow human beings and are merely 'connecting' as components of a system. I find that very sad.

> Please, listen to what you are reading.

> Yours sincerely,"

The reply from 'Jim' while it sends regrets and good wishes concludes by expressing sadness at "the tone of your letter" and makes no attempt at all to address the serious issues about communication made in it.

A small story indeed and one which could be replicated a thousand times no doubt, if seldom with such a telling response to the lost opportunity of a real human exchange.

All true exchanges, all real meetings of their very nature take place in a kind of No Man's Land. They cannot be entered into if at all costs a state of security must be preserved. Heads have to be put over parapets, risks must be taken. You give something of yourself when you say a thank you from the heart. It might not be received by the heart, it might be pushed back in your teeth, or greeted with complete indifference. The Trust has covered itself with its apparently adequate thank you letter. It might even claim to have kept to the spirit of its mission statement, displayed on the bottom of its notepaper that it is an *"Investor in People"* (whatever that may mean). What it has actually done is merely satisfy appearances, which in one way is to have done everything, in another nothing.

At any given time in a society's life there seem invariably to be a few phrases around which brook no denial, and which are very handy for people to seize upon and use when they want to make a fine impression. One that has lasted for a substantial stretch of my lifetime (I would like to think it will soon be put to rest, though I doubt it) goes like this, *"Justice must not only be done, it must be seen to be done"*. Fine phrases such as this, unexceptionable in themselves, when they have turned irreversibly into clichés become impressively fertile; the following could readily be amongst their many offspring: *"Proper accountability must not only be put in place it must be seen to have been put in place"*. The trouble is, of course, that the more determined people are that something must be seen to be the case the more likely they are to set up systems to make absolutely sure that it jolly well will be seen to be the case. Whether the real thing itself, true Justice, proper Accountablity, or whatever else, actually survives the process is another matter altogether. Anyone who doesn't know how easily appearances can come to matter vastly more than reality knows very little about the world and very little about themselves either.

Concentrating on appearances does of course have a great deal going for it. If the appearances are all in place hands can be held high and shown to be spotlessly clean. Inspectors, complainants, protesters, interviewers, should they appear, can all be shown the clean hands and then shown the door, and if the worst has come to the worst, those who invoke the law and bring actions against you very probably won't win them. In the long run, though, the disadvantages are of a quite different order of importance, and the supreme disadvantage is that No Man's Land, that place where true encounter is possible, where people learn to see each other aright and learn to trust each other and offer and admire the family photos, slips away out of sight and mind, lest occasionally the infuriated recipient of a formal thank you letter, say, should cry out to be heard and met as a fellow human being.

No one can ever enter No Man's Land in complete security, no one can ever call it their own and claim possession of it. The easy thing to do certainly is to draw up clear boundary lines either side of it, throw up impenetrable barriers, allow no access to it, and even, as may well happen over time, come to disbelieve its very existence, both to oneself and to whatever others may be on the other side of it.

At this point a couple of quotations from applications for jobs, one ancient, one modern. Most of us know what it is like trying to put such a thing together, no good standing back like a shrinking violet, not these days anyway it seems. The modern one sets out as follows, *"I feel I am very well suited to the position in that I meet all the essential and desirable criteria in the person specification."* He goes on to say why this is so in impressive detail and concludes, *"I have therefore all the skills and abilities relevant to this position."* At first I was surprised when I read this to find myself so strikingly reminded of Johann Sebastian Bach's letter to the Duke of Saxony, to be found at the front of my copy of the *B Minor Mass* (a work of art which has been called the *"greatest of all times and all peoples"*), when he too was after a job. He sent along the Kyrie and Gloria of the later completed Mass to help his cause, and writes as follows, "I lay before your Kingly Majesty this trifling proof of the science which I have been able to attain in music, with the very humble petition that you will be pleased to regard it, not according to the measure of the meanness of the composition, but with a gracious eye, as befits your Majesty's world-famed clemency, and condescend to take me under your Majesty's most mighty protection."

Both letters, of course, exemplify the conventions pertaining to the time of writing, and in themselves tell us virtually nothing about their writers; countless others from the early 21st century and the mid 18th century might have been found. What is interesting is not the obvious differences but the similarity. Both conventions require a tacit denial of any real meeting ground, the one is all pseudo confidence, the other all pseudo humility. Nothing the matter with either convention in itself, everything the matter when either comes to be taken seriously, in which case No Man's Land is eclipsed and in its place appears a phenomenon as dubious as a 'person specification'. Any decent job selector, of course, takes the letter of application for the piece of convention that it is, and then sets about trying to throw light on to No Man's Land so that there will be a place where applicant and selector can meet as 'fellow human beings'. It is hard to do that though, and the task is certainly made no easier by the hard self sell required by contemporary convention. Often enough it simply isn't done, which one knows to be the case by the frequency with which one hears remarks such as, "so and so got the job because they performed so well on the day". They too took along their Kyrie and Gloria in the form of some striking presentation perhaps. Where there is no adequate No Man's Land in which to meet as fellow human beings appearances and performances are bound to reign supreme. No one can feel truly at ease in such a world, there is nowhere to be truly at ease when all the boundary lines are rigidly in place and the barriers have been built up firm and solid.

It is striking how small things of no apparent importance at the time sometimes stick in the mind for the rest of a lifetime. I remember when I had just started teaching, more than 40 years ago now, being told by my ever optimistic and cheerful flatmate that he'd just met our senior master (not his, he taught at a different school). *"He's a great guy that Doc Barker,"* he said. I think he had met him after a game at some clubhouse event, he was a great rugby player. To a newcomer like myself the Doc Barker in question was one of those eternal figures who had been teaching history at the school more or less since the thing itself had begun. I didn't think he was a great guy at all, not least because he was so disconcerting. So far as I could see, and I may well have been seeing partially, he was totally fortified by gown, notes, reputation and formidable presence. There was no No Man's Land where people met as fellow human beings in the staffroom, or in his classes, that I got any hint of. Why he in particular should stand for me as the type of the formal, unapproachable teacher I don't know. It was probably unjust, and if he were that type I have met plenty of others before and since. Perhaps it was simply because my flatmate called him *"a great guy,"* and the phrase jarred so. Great guys, teachers, counsellors, doctors, or whatever are very well capable of coming out unarmed from behind the parapets and taking the risk of meeting others in that uncertain place over which no one has complete control and of which no one can claim the ownership. I think I knew that then as well as I know it now.

I was talking to one ex-colleague not long ago, one who may deserve the description that Doc Barker in my view didn't deserve, and in the course of conversation he referred to his recent visit to an educational institution as their external examiner. No one playing such a role, or meeting someone else doing so, can be sure beforehand that the barriers will be removed and the boundaries crossed sufficiently for there to be a real encounter in a No Man's Land over which neither claims power or possession. To a large extent it is the one who most obviously appears to be master of the situation who must take the first steps into that uncertain terrain. Indeed being equal to taking risks of that kind is clearly one of the prerequisites of decent leadership. It doesn't necessarily require that much provided what is offered is the real thing. *"I told them what a really demanding and difficult job they were having to do and how well they were doing it,"* he said. Nothing much in itself and obviously no magic password into the terrain. Clearly here, however, what was said was meant and was received as such. Straight away the sort of atmosphere starts to develop in which people can begin to meet each other properly and get into something worthwhile instead of the mere appearance of it. It was striking to meet him a few weeks later in a state, rare for him, of some considerable irritation. His own institution had just been the subject of an inspection and the person looking at his field of work, perhaps in part because she knew that he sometimes played the inspector role himself, had at one moment invited what appeared to be a real exchange in No Man's Land by sharing very specific perceptions about the serious dangers of falsity and unreality that exist for all parties in an inspection, only at the next moment to reassert full power over and possession of the terrain. The full range of inspectorial demands was suddenly and peremptorily required, and it was as if the earlier exchanges, with their insights and subtleties had been as nothing, and could be wiped out with no harm done. It is indeed irritating, having read the signals as best one can, to find oneself in No Man's Land with a bottle of beer, the family photos and a makeshift football, and then discover that one's expected partner is back behind his parapet sending up Very lights and pulling the pins out of grenades with his teeth.

I wonder if in this age we really are more assailed by invitations to hazardous self-exposure in No Man's Land than our forebears were. All those letters, for example, addressed to us by name, telling us how valued or how generous we are, or how we in particular have been found worthy of a special reward, they do flood through the letter-box; and who doesn't sometimes find a smile of accidental mutuality freezing on their lips when invited by a face on a screen to come and join in such and such a TV jollification? And am I the only one who has to struggle sometimes with an ancient anxiety about discourtesy when I put the phone down halfway through a recorded speech apparently saying thank you to me personally for using this or that facility? Our old video recorder used to wish us good morning and goodbye. Happily the new one doesn't. What stuff and nonsense it all is, and mostly laughable, yet how insidious it can be too as a substitute for real connection. An old man I know, recently bereaved, fell for it so impressively that he got to telling people all about his new friend so and so, who kept writing to him as 'Dear George', and to whom he really enjoyed writing back. It was some while before interested parties found out that George's new friend had induced him into parting with much of his savings for this or that excellent reason. Recourse to law, which by its nature is not easily enticed into No Man's Land, did recoup some of the losses.

No Man's Land is not only dangerous to those enticed into it to be damaged or fleeced, there is plenty of risk involved in stepping into it with one's eyes wide open and signalling to others to join one there. I illustrate that with what is again a very slight thing on the face of it, though I still carry some discomfort from the transaction. I used to have to do quite a lot of interviewing of students hoping to become teachers. Most of my interviewing experience had been with post graduates, I had become less used to 18 year olds and I deserve to carry my share of responsibility for the mess this interview turned into. Not many 18 year olds, though, are so completely packaged. It was not just the outward appearance, she was clearly entirely well trained, presumably by teachers and parents, to remain absolutely behind the parapets, revealing not a thing. What I was trying to do was get a sufficient hint that behind all that protection there was a person who did understand at least something of the inevitable exposure and risk involved in real learning. It ended in total failure with each of us feeling a different kind of despair. One might argue that I should have given up the struggle before we reached that point. I don't think so myself, since an interview over something as important as training to be a teacher in which no real meeting takes place does seem a ridiculous nonsense, for all that it may not be an infrequent one. I think I should have been able to encourage her into No Man's Land and that it was worth every effort to do so, but that on the day, for whatever reason, I didn't manage it. I offered her a place because the appearances and qualifications were after all impeccable, and who was I to be so arrogant as to be sure there wasn't a person behind it all who could learn to be the real thing as a teacher? A letter came from the school complaining of new, strange, unfair interviewing techniques evidently in use that they knew nothing about, unfair presumably because they hadn't had a chance to train their students to see them coming and learn the defence techniques required to neutralise them.

It is very easy indeed to shoot people down in No Man's Land and very easy to be shot down, which is presumably why politicians stick to agreed formulae, gibes at the opposition and planned sound bites, when confronted by interviewers apparently bent on luring them into the danger zone where they may more easily be shown up as the stereotypical charlatans and tricksters they, not surprisingly, come to be expected to be. It is also, presumably, in part why the brain surgeon, say, may decide not to operate, even when the chances of success seem good to him, if he thinks that, while the patient's brain might perforce have to meet him in that uncertain No Man's Land, the rest of him, and his lawyers too, might be very firmly entrenched on their side of the lines, ready to throw legislative grenades if the brain doesn't come back in pristine condition. The terrain can be just as dangerous for the teacher or the counsellor, or the nurse, the social worker and the priest. Keep the boundaries skills well polished, don't take unnecessary risks. Do the job as well as you can of course, but only in terms of what's been negotiated and fixed beforehand. Client, pupil, patient, parishioner may indeed have fallen among thieves, but don't go over the top and start playing Good Samaritan. And whatever else you do at all costs don't pick up or put your arms around the lost and crying child.

The snag is of course that to remain armed and invulnerable behind one's lines of defence and to refuse or neglect opportunities to meet anyone or anything in No Man's Land does not actually lead to safety for any of the parties involved.

The politician and his opponent or interviewer bandying 'when did you stop beating your wife?' questions and sound bite replies, for example, metamorphose into marionettes which we turn away from in disgust, and worse still the language itself becomes a discredited medium; as if nothing worth the saying could be said in it; as if there were no medium in which dialogue could take place; as if even the idea of dialogue itself might be an illusion, and only fudge and fixing a reality. Things are no better for the brain surgeon and his patient, or for the teacher, priest and social worker, and most assuredly they are no better for the lost and crying child. If people never learn and are encouraged not to learn that the really worthwhile and important things in life are always done in No Man's Land, the one and only place of true conversation; that risks have to be taken; outcomes cannot be foretold; a measure of faith is an absolute prerequisite, then we too might just as well sing the song of ultimate pointlessness and futility that the troops sometimes sang in the Great War on their way up the line:

"We're here because we're here because we're here because we're here..."

A certain uneasiness comes over me as I embark on another apparently trivial recollection. The awestruck Edgar's words at the end of the tragedy of *King Lear* have always struck a powerful chord with me:

"The oldest hath borne most: we that are young
Shall never see so much, nor live so long."

It sometimes feels like that in relation to past generations, and especially so perhaps to one such as myself who, if just able to remember the start of the second of the last century's two great wars, was far too young ever to be frightened by it, and who timed his middle years very nicely to match the full blossoming of the Welfare State. Yet to a degree it could be that it is the very slightness of the stories that may help them to illuminate my theme better than more apparently impressive ones might. After all for most of us most of our lives' transactions are not that evidently dramatic, but that doesn't make them any the less striking and significant for those who experience them.

Twice in my life I have had a real problem trying to get through an open door. Once I didn't make it, that's when I was teaching on supply, the class of 37 small children I referred to in the first section, six year olds they were mostly, and me trained only for 11-18's. It wasn't that I was frightened to go through the door, though after a few days on my own with the class I had become reduced to a state of almost complete cluelessness as to what to do if I did get through it. Maybe it was simply that that finished me off. I could neither, like old Doc Barker with his gown, notes and reputation, exude dangerousness from the front line trenches, nor, in like case to my old Sheffield friend with the class of spastics, could I muster the powers necessary to draw the children into No Man's Land and meet them there, as my old English teacher had been able to do, for enough of us anyway, with his reading of *Sohrab and Rustum*. The Head-mistress was sympathetic and good natured and made me cups of tea, and very soon after I managed to get myself some supply work in a secondary school.

The occasion when I did just manage to get through the door took place quite a few years later. It was in the '70's, at a time when there was lots of change and reorganisation going on in further education (plus ça change ...). It was a time of mergers, takeovers, rationalisations and redundancies. The air was full of noises, and full of apprehension. When the dust settled in our corner up here in the north I found myself, with some of my past colleagues, part of an institution new to us, which had by now more than tripled its size after a series of mergers, and of takeovers in all but name. Naturally there were lots of meetings held to try to sort out the future. There was little enough of climbing over the parapets to meet each other though. Signals did occasionally get waved but it seemed too risky for much notice to be taken of them. For the most part we behaved as if there were no such place as a No Man's Land in which we needed to be meeting each other.

It wasn't anybody's fault, it would have taken exceptional leadership and a lot of courage and forbearance on everyone's part for things to have been much different. The consequences were none the less serious though, and the future life of the institution remained dogged by problems that could only have been resolved by genuine forays into No Man's Land; disappointments, misunderstandings, suspicions and fears lived on intact. Perhaps we were afraid that the terrain was just too well mined and none of us wanted to be the first to parade such a fear in public.

For my part anyway the first year in the new set up was often very unpleasant, and I well remember the couple of occasions when it felt as if there were an impenetrable barrier across the entrance into the buildings where I worked. It took me all the willpower I possessed to force myself through that curious block. Looking back on it now, I'm sure it was because I had come to despair of ever again meeting a colleague there and being able to lower the defences and say how things really were. When and how that eventually did happen, and two of us read and responded to each other's signals I can't exactly remember. One of us must have been the first to say something unrepeatable, most probably in connection with the latest ghastly, vacuous meeting. Which of us it was I have no idea. What I do remember very well, though, is the laughter and elation that accompanied our subsequent rapid fire exchange of perceptions about the institution and the astonishing goings on in it. To be able to share one's vision of things at last, and to find out that it was far from being some private nightmare was an enormous relief and immensely energising. I doubt very much either whether such an experience is as uncommon as might at first be imagined. Anyway, there were no further problems after that with apparently impassable thresholds.

At the same time as all that was happening I had just become a counsellor for the organisation that was later to become Relate, and I had to attend regular meetings there too in order to discuss the work. The difference was astonishing. It wasn't thanks to anything especially wonderful about counsellors, it was just that the assumption underlying the whole enterprise was that there was no sensible place in which to meet other than No Man's Land. If we couldn't encounter each other undefended there it wasn't going to be worth encountering each other at all. No good talking about the work and trying to find out how to do it better, how to understand clients and our attitudes towards them and so on, if we behaved like those splendid chaps in Rider Haggard's *King Solomon's Mines*, who, as Graham Greene has it, would only ever admit to a fault in order to show how it might be overcome. There were of course the odd counsellors who did adopt such tactics, but they could at least be told what they were up to, and even if they couldn't altogether see it they weren't able to do too much damage.

My point is not at all that it is lots nicer kicking a ball about in No Man's Land, though it certainly is; it is that it's incomparably more useful and effective. No Man's Land is the place where things are not merely *seen* to be done (sometimes indeed they might not be, matters are not cut and dried in there and the perspectives can magnify enormously), it is the place where they *are* done.

I don't think I have ever felt more like the archetypal first world consumer than I did a few years ago on the Canarian island of La Gomera when, having swum nonchalantly the length of the hotel pool in hot sunshine, I sat down on a kind of toadstool some few inches below the water line and ordered a midday drink from a bar placed to serve torsos lapped by the warm blue water (the nonchalance, or rather the attempt at an appearance of it, being my usual effort to disguise a pathetic swimming stroke). It was an odd place in which to get into a rage about schools and inspections, which happened thanks to my getting into conversation with an equally half submerged couple. The lady was a teacher of the no-nonsense school – "good thing these Ofsted inspections, sorts the wheat from the chaff, keeps everybody up to the mark", that kind of thing. After a few attempts at counter arguments (one isn't at one's most imposing sitting on a toadstool in old fashioned bathing trunks) I bottled up the rage and we moved on to safer, more touristy topics.

I'm sure that was one of the moments in which this book had its genesis. I still think that the anger I felt, which was not incidentally directed at the person sitting half submerged beside me, was profoundly justified, but in that situation arguments, even if backed up by impressive tales of damage done to people and institutions, clearly weren't going to get me anywhere. If I were to come up with something that would really have a chance of convincing those not already convinced, I would have to think a lot deeper and work a lot harder than I could possibly do under a tropical sun, supping a midday beer.

Whether the lady I met at that curious bar would have been at all impressed by what I have written so far I have no idea. If she does chance to read this she might well not recognise either of us, since my anger did remain largely invisible and my arguments cut no ice (the little there was of that commodity was cut up ready to be dropped into the drinks). Maybe at this point, however, some kind of direct confrontation might be in order. How is it that, in the face of all those sensible seeming, even overdue measures that I referred to at the start of this section; getting more regulation into systems; improving accountability; instituting formal qualifications; setting up supervisory bodies, and so on, all quite clearly matters which can play an important part in improving education, health and counselling services and the like, how is it that in the light of all this to be angry and upset might sometimes be entirely the right and proper reaction?

Everything I have written so far has, I hope, some contribution to make towards an answer to that question. A summary, however, might go like this. Of course people should be angry and upset whenever they encounter behaviours and activities which, in Wittgenstein's terms, appear to know nothing about the existence of that second part, the important one; which, in Tolstoy's terms, speak only of and to the *"narrow, material something"*, which all of us are, and which exclude and by implication deny the *"infinitely great and illimitable existing within"* us; which, in Buber's terms, speak only in the language of the Primary Word I-It, and address the other as nothing but an object to be known, checked up on, and managed and manipulated when necessary; an object which could not possibly be thought of as being required to do something so remote and fanciful as gather *"the child's presence into his or her store as one of the hearers of his or her communion with the world"*. In the face of behaviours, activities and measures in which possibility in people is unrecognised, faith in them neither understood nor practised, and in which No Man's Land lies waste and unexplored, how can we easily be forgiven for not being angry and upset? These are precisely the conditions in which appearances are able and prone to ease out reality, and in which lies and nonsense prosper with busy enthusiasm.

"I am becoming more and more conscious of the 'management of appearances' creeping into every aspect of working life," a friend writes. Teacher trainees it seems are all (no exceptions) to be formally tested so that it can be shown that they have competence in maths, literacy and ICT (as if, apart from the latter, such requirements were something new, or as if, thanks to them, never again could anything remotely akin to a Wackford Squeers slip through the system). So a lot of money is spent, many additional man hours required, measures and machinery put in place. "All the paperwork and rhetoric is very officious," my correspondent writes, and I quote – "It is mandatory that before your testing centre can be 'activated', that at least one member of staff is a qualified (and here a six letter acronymic) Testing Administrator," and it goes on at some length in similar manner. "When I talk to them on the phone, though, it is extraordinarily casual and friendly." He asks about Invigilation, "Well, the students are supposed to be invigilated but as long as someone can glance through a glass partition now and again that's fine." And the qualified Administrator to be? "Oh, send anyone along and they can train up other people."

So long as the system is in place and things can be seen to be being done, what does it matter what is actually done or not done?

As for the 'A' levels, those tests so vital to school leavers, especially those hoping to go on to further education, the average of the grades gets better every year, doesn't it? Really? Every year? And for ever and ever? Such an impressive and fine appearance does give us all a warm glow when we hear the item getting its annual headline treatment by the media; for about three seconds that is, by which time most of us have blinked and woken up. And those forms I occasionally have to complete in my supervisor role, to support counsellors as part of their increasingly obligatory and ever more frequently required applications for membership of a national supervisory body, which is presumably thought to be doing a necessary and useful job, I might just as well be writing to the Duke of Saxony myself. It is all style and appearance. A number of people earn money training counsellors to get the appearance and manner of their application just right, as of course do people helping schools and teachers to get the documentation spot on prior to an Ofsted inspection – all rather like the public letter writers of some ancient far away bazaar, who knew just the language to use to get things nicely fixed. And another small example here of that invidious requirement for the management of appearances. In amongst all the answers that the form of application to that supervisory body requires a counsellor's supervisor such as myself to come up with, would I ever really say "No" in answer to the question as to whether the counsellor has read theorganisation's Code of Ethics? "Have you?" I ask, "Yes", says the counsellor, I write 'yes' in the gap provided, they presumably say, *"Jolly good"*, and we're all as happy as can be.

"What do we expect when we are in despair and go to a man?" So Buber's resounding question, and the answer is something rather more than a smart manager of appearances, who may or may not have read some Code of Ethics; and the same applies across the board. We expect, or rather hope against hope for, someone whose ethical sense is so richly developed that they really do know what it is to be the bearer of another's communion with the world (however they might express that idea). What do we hope for in our heart of hearts when, ourselves heartbroken, we write to an employee of the NHS asking about the latter days of a partner who has died of cancer? Hardly a reply explaining the Pathway to Death that the loved one was skilfully moved along. What do we hope for when we go to the hospital needing surgery, or the hospice with only weeks or days left to live? Less drastically, maybe, but still vitally, what do we hope for and need, when we start school or go to college, or when people come to inspect our work? What is it that we invariably hope for and need at those times when the fundamental unsafeness of life is more starkly apparent to us than it is in the usual day to day run of things? I have said enough I think about what we do not want and need; Martin Buber's way of expressing what it is we do need seems to me as good as any, that presence, namely, *"by means of which we are told nevertheless there is meaning"*. Good Samaritans, to express the idea another way, will do just as well, those that is, who come the crunch are not hemmed in by the regulations and do not rest content with their mastery of the Boundaries Skills, but will meet us in No Man's Land when that is where we need to be met, wherever No Man's Land may chance to be: in a surgeon's office; a hospital ward; a counsellor's room; a corridor; not to mention any other place in which we might find ourselves if we are anxious and afraid, or if we have fallen among thieves and been wounded, physically or psychologically, and left, one way or another, like the man in the parable, half dead.

We can meet each other properly in places such as these when we are capable of putting aside the apparatus for the management of appearances, and our sense of the other as nothing but an Other. We have no way of doing it if we have no sense of the other's Possibility, *"of the infinitely great and illimitable existing within"* people. We can do it only when we live with sufficient faith in ourselves and others to be able to dispense, at times and for long enough, with that *"irritable reaching after fact and reason"* that Keats speaks of, and so are able to do without the flimsy sustenance of a false conviction that the world is really a safe and manageable place in which to live after all.

That "all shall be well, and all manner of things shall be well" is not a dogmatic belief to be asserted, it is a testimony which is sometimes revealed by and to people in their living and working amongst one another. To experience such testimony being endangered or damaged by any behaviours and activities, however apparently well intentioned, ought indeed to make us extremely angry and upset. We cannot hope to encounter anything in our dealings with each other which is richer to us than such testimony, nor anything of which we are so profoundly in need.

Voices: Richard Carr

**Richard Carr has taught Drama and English in schools
and colleges in the north east. Much of his spare time
is spent in youth theatre, and he has been involved in
local productions as both writer and director. His additional
interests include philosophy and the work of P.G. Wodehouse;
he writes about these and more.**

1. The Conversation.

I can think of three good reasons for not reading essays like this, particularly if
they are intensely personal. They may be drearily disaffected; they are often
drearily self-justifying; and they often terminate in a featureless morass called
Stress. Other kinds of publication to do with that great topic of our time,
Education, have related, though apparently contrary, failings. Collections of
articles from research institutions and pieces perpetrated by the QCA, the DfE,
or an LEA have all the spontaneous humanity and depth of an I-speak-your-
weight machine or a message from outer space. They lack the ability to be
connected with, as do the disaffected or self-justifying articles and memoirs.
Even if the motive for reading is to seek a little company in one's disaffection,
self-justification or stress, reading or writing such pieces is, unfortunately, very
unlikely to lead anywhere that leads anywhere else.

It is very unlikely to lead to a conversation, for instance. What would be much
more likely is a simple alternation of monologues. Exchange, interplay, the
growth of understanding, sudden clarities – not likely at all. So why do
monologues happen so often? The answer, I think, must be that they can very
readily be deployed either as defences against risk or as somewhat belated
attempts to have a voice in a conversation that has passed one by.

Conversation is a risk in the sense that it cannot be foreseen or accounted for
beforehand, nor can it truly be at the direction of ulterior motives. It is, indeed,
potentially far more riskily but satisfyingly creative than we are often able to
imagine. Conversation's freedom, endlessness and variety are even the terms
under which the philosopher Michael Oakeshott is able to discuss virtually the
whole of human mental activity.

> *"As civilised human beings, we are the inheritors, neither of an inquiry about
> ourselves and the world, nor of an accumulating body of information, but of a
> conversation, begun in the primeval forests and extended and made more
> articulate in the course of centuries ... of course there is argument, inquiry*

and information, but wherever these are profitable they are recognised as passages in this conversation, and perhaps they are not the most captivating of the passages. It is the ability to participate in this conversation, and not the ability to reason cogently, to make discoveries about the world, or to continue a better world, which distinguishes the human being from the animal. It is this conversation which, in the end, gives place and character to every human activity and utterance ... and the final measure of intellectual achievement is in terms of its contribution to the conversation in which all universes of discourse meet." [1]

This intensely hopeful and tonic passage has been quoted at length because it contains with some ease the full scope of what I intend to discuss. Its tonic quality lies in the facts that the Conversation is strictly unstoppable, that we all have a place within it, and that we are in touch by virtue of our humanity with all the other contributors. This unending human communion is the sole, but sufficient, guarantee of whatever reality human utterance can achieve. It is not subordinate to inquiry, discovery, or progress. It is not capable of finality, since its being is simply to continue, to affiliate, and to grant power. It is not the subject of any aim or purpose, and it is not, strictly, an object for thought at all. Conversation, to cite Oakeshott once more, "is not an enterprise designed to yield an extrinsic profit, nor is it an activity of exegesis; it is an unrehearsed intellectual adventure". As it is neither subjective nor objective, but rather something prior to both, it's only by virtue of this Conversation that we recognise each other as beings of the same kind, and participants in each other's being.

We do, of course, live out our lives in the sight of this truth, and act with great urgency and passion in the awareness of it. If that weren't so, we would not be able to fall in love, to care, or to delight in each other at all, and nor would we so unfailingly think of our lives in terms of intermingled stories, nor imagine the past and the future in ways which make narrative sense. Because we *can* do that, it allows us to grant others a place in the story of ourselves and a reality quite different from that of mere figures in the landscape.

But our necessary faith in the Conversation can be damaged, more perhaps by anxiety than by barbarism or violence. I think it's being damaged at this moment by developments in the management of our living, and of our making a living.

Every age has a deposit of lurid examples of the Conversation being blithely forgotten or traduced, and even of its being deliberately effaced – inhumanity of all kinds seeming to be so perversely undertaken in full consciousness of what it is that is sinned against. Why this should be so is perhaps a question for psychology (although literature is more likely to treat it with the open-ended thoroughness it deserves). Despite the wanton destructiveness of such things, however, humanity has always survived them, and continues to; indeed, it may even thrive on opposition to them (eg in Belsen or Rwanda).

So it may be that a greater threat to the Conversation is the outbreak of an everyday failure of nerve. We don't always easily forge again our trust in the world that meets us after our birth and our early feelings, as a commentator on Freud put it, of "oceanic omnipotence", and nor is our faith in the Conversation always confirmed as we grow or maintained as we decline. Such veniality is always incident to human affairs: breaches of trust, boredom, anxiety, vengefulness – fleeting betrayals, possibly, but cumulative in their effect.

Is such an erosion beginning to be evident in human affairs – eg in personal relationships, and more specifically in relationships to do with education – at the moment? Despite our sense, perhaps, of a greater *vividness* in relationships compared with (say) the Edwardian era, and despite our much greater temptation to assert the valuable in such things, I think it could be claimed that many people are aware, at some level, of fault-lines beneath the surface. That is what this essay is about.

2. The Conversation in fragments.

Faith can be stunted or overborne in other ways, for instance by confusion. This is particularly so in an era of such breathtaking complexity as ours. Human conversation is, and has been for some time, so beset by a panoply of problematising factors that it is difficult to characterise: there are so many calls on our attention, and yet so much necessary indifference to our own calls, so much ease of communication on the one hand and so much intractable difficulty of what has come to be called 'getting through' on the other that the Conversation is in danger of being occluded by its fragments. Meeting each other's reality, and letting it weigh equally with our own simultaneously-felt reality, has been 'problematised' by the sheer range and variety of the calls we receive, and the calls we feel ourselves bound to make or cannot help making. They succeed each other with a bewildering, flickering rapidity that can cause a kind of self-protective film to descend over one's receptivity. What other age has populated itself with so many brightening, fading, competing and insecure signals? The clutter of effect one meets in, say, a trip through a department store, an evening watching television, or working in even a middle-sized organisation, is simply staggering; disorientating, potentially. It is clear that such calls on us, and the calls we reciprocally make, are legion. Perhaps it will not be rash to suggest that they do something quite unsettling to our sense of ourselves, to our 'self-image', to use a highly revealing modern coinage. Is it even possible that this problematic 'image' is what we have where previous civilisations had 'soul'?

Our 'faith in the Conversation' would be disturbed by this because our unsettled mentality is its locus – we both find ourselves within the Conversation, and are the means of its continuance. The more our sense of communicative centrality is disturbed, the more subject to interference, to not-quite-humanised ambiguity, our living in Conversation becomes. We may become prone to accepting substitutes for it, which amounts to placing our faith in fragments of it, or to denying it altogether. The comforting feelings that there are no loopholes in our lives, that the hatches are battened down, that we have everything *listed* and *tabulated*, that our *systems* are *sensitive*, that we at least can't be caught out by Confusion, can quite readily offer themselves as substitutes. This would be the face that anxiety turns to the world – its reflective surface. Surfaces, and the anxiety they screen, are much in evidence, as I shall try to show. Conversation is fractured in such states of mind.

This is why writing about education in terms only of disaffection or stress leads nowhere. For one thing, it marginalises itself, and becomes a self-protective monologue; for another, it is nonchalantly trounced by another kind of monologue, that kind of complacent and unchallengeable sign-language which we associate with national decision-makers cautiously addressing the nation.

The discussion of any national concern, either from inside or outside, is bedevilled by the fact that what one has to say comes (partly) from somewhere political, travels to somewhere political, can be said to serve interests at bottom political, and so can easily be deflected or marginalised. There is no such thing as 'writing white' in education; to use another motif from cultural analysis, one's most searching and heartfelt truths are, once in the public domain, "always-already" enlisted politically. In this case, resistance to one's-own-truth is couched in terms of an accusation that one is refusing to accept the challenge, to adapt to change, to understand accountability, flexible working, and raising of standards. Any teacher who focuses, for instance, on 'stress' is instantly kebabbed on one of these lethal *chevaux-de-frises*. The alternative is marginalising. Exhibition of one's views on such little stages as union magazines, poetry circles, or, under a pseudonym, the weekend edition of *The Guardian*, is therefore legitimate, perhaps even welcome. There no damage is done. It has been guided into an eternal self-reflexive loop and gone beyond.

Kebabbing and marginalising between them render the whole concept of public debate illusory. There *is* no public debate about education despite (or indeed because of) the incessant harping upon education as a national priority. When there is no longer a space for debate (and spaces are what we will come to at the end of this essay), or a truly common ground, a stylisation of voice is forced upon one which almost defines in advance what one has to say, and which encourages monologue. Auden expresses this with great fineness in the dedicatory poem ('To Reinhold and Ursula Niebuhr') in *Nones*:

> *"No civil style survived*
> *That pandemonium*
> *But the wry, the sotto-voce,*
> *Ironic, and monochrome;*
> *And where should we find shelter*
> *For joy or mere content*
> *When little was left standing*
> *But the suburb of dissent."*

This sense of a language lost or shattered into mannerism is a shadowy and worry-producing awareness that stands alongside what we say when we feel our saying is called-for, when we feel we are on stage having received our cue and the audience is waiting. Such mannerism being easily available to us is, perhaps, evidence that at some level we are aware of the imperilled condition of 'debate'. It may mean, for us of the internet generation, that ease, and compulsiveness, of communication are eating away at reality of communication. For teachers, it means that one's own voice is only precariously one's own, and becomes mannerism in the very effort to be heard – the mannerism, that is to say, of one consciously aping or denying orthodoxy.

To be exiled to the "suburb of dissent" not only bars one from the fulfilment of what one has to say, (precludes entering the Conversation, that is), but in so deforming at the start one's consciousness of the possibility of fulfilment carves one's voice into styles which are by definition excluding or excluded.

3. Maxims and Signs.

It seems to me that since the outmoding (not the resolution) of the old political certainties of the left and right, which were themselves admittedly stylised, and despite the multitude of voices surrounding us, there has resulted a great public silence, a Nothing, an absence of encounter. What we have now is orthodoxy, which by a breathtaking irony is anything but static and marmoreal - it is *protean*, reshaping itself continuously - and a host of little piping voices in the wilderness. All possible shades of political or religious opinion, an uncoordinated cacophony of voices of the previously-dispossessed [2], an eruption of barely-possible voices and other kinds ranging from the laudable to the ludicrous are now to be heard, all of them calling on us to ally ourselves to and through them, encouraging us to *define* ourselves with their help: to announce ourselves. Many of them feel the urge to translate their sense of the competing pressure of other voices into, for instance, the act of 'making a statement', another revealing coinage. Making a statement is now a forlorn if vigorously-prosecuted act of a kind we have become very familiar with, an act, like the mission statement, which says a great deal more about its maker than its maker thinks it does. The maker of statements is attempting belatedly to join a public realm in a very defensive manner: the statement is their armour, their credentials for doing so, and I would say that the fact of it being made is far more important than its content, which is perhaps necessarily vague and of a smooth, soapy or suety texture, enabling it to insert itself easily into the crowded public airwaves. I remember, some years ago, thinking that the pinnacle of statement-making had been reached when I heard, on a late-night current-affairs programme, a naked interviewee in a Paris nightclub saying she was *"making a statement about having a good time"*. Is it significant that such statements seem to preclude or acknowledge as [3] irrelevant older-fashioned concepts such as 'argument' or 'discussion'? It is as if there are now only positions to be occupied, rather than adventures of discovery to be followed.

At last, we have all been given a voice, with the startling proviso that all of us have simultaneously been stricken deaf. We can't attend to all the calls on us, patently; a perhaps more worrying thing is that even the calls on us which we would like to attend to may feel, at times, infected with the same kind of unreality as the thousands of calls we are aware don't reach us. Coleridge (in *On the Constitution of the Church and State*) foresaw one result of this: "A swarm of clever, well-informed men: an anarchy of minds, a despotism of maxims"; Henri Lefebvre (in *Everyday Life in the Modern World*) observed emptiness surrounding us, but *"an emptiness filled with signs"*, which include what I have phrased as 'calls upon us'. The maxims and the signs are what we have instead of public encounter.

Maxims, signs, lists, tabulations, statements, beliefs which we Stand Up for, these are all signals of *finality*: signals that the I which accedes to them is stable, univocal, definite, *real* – *"foursquare to every wind that blows"*, in the words of my old school song. There is a character in Kingsley Amis' brilliant and politically incorrect novel *Jake's Thing* who exemplifies this. Geoffrey Mabbott, whose utterly indeterminate trade is that of buyer for a chutney firm, reveals at a therapy group how it gradually dawned on him that all his opinions, beliefs, evidences of individuality, were simply "things he said so as to seem to be someone." [4] At the end of this confession,

> *"Geoffrey was thanked for his efforts rather as if he had just failed an audition by a small but distinct margin. Poor old bugger, Jake thought to himself, at*

least you're a cut above Miss Calvert [one of his students] and that lot. To them, the failure of things like knowledge to win their interest constituted a grave if not fatal defect in the thing itself." (Ch.15)

The result is that, this being the first thing he has genuinely noticed about himself or anybody else, Geoffrey is able to jettison the lot and start again, without much hope but with the entirely wonderful achievement of being able to distinguish between what he genuinely feels and what he genuinely doesn't. (It is the much more intelligent, observant and individual Jake who, at the end of the novel, is cut off, by his own choice, from the richness of living). Geoffrey points up the possibility that a good deal of the time we actually don't have this newly-innocent confidence. Instead we may substitute prematurely-finalised versions of ourselves and the things we believe in, and indulge in judging and categorising because they make us seem to be someone.

4. Resuscitating Encounter.

Genuine encounter would be seriously disturbing to this feeling. It does not anxiously see its end in its beginning, and it is not capable of being surrounded, hollowed out, and reduced to a grading by Judgment. Judgment in the light of encounter seems pitifully weak, anxious, paltry and unaware of its own rationale. I simply do not believe, either, that the way the world edged onward through the millennia has anything to do with that kind of closed analytic. It is much more reasonable, and evident, that a gradual accumulation of tricks, wrinkles, stories, rituals, memories and rules of thumb created the human world: abstraction, perfection and certainty didn't. The kind of mentality which so overvalues Judgment is, I'd say, comparatively recent in human history. It results in overemphatic, overcommunicative, proliferating fields of discourse struggling for mastery, well-buttressed monologues (cf., in the words of E.M. Forster, "poor little talkative Christianity"). Such a mentality is oxymoronic, niggling and yet sweeping, defensive and yet aggressive, stuffed full of experience and history and yet always premature, cunning and yet shallow and untutored, like a Nazi ambassador.

Are there really people like this, though? I should say no, not as such. If there were, I would be subjecting *them* to a simple and seductive judgment. But there are states of mind like this, and practices which imply it. There are people (ourselves) who are sometimes subject to them, and some of us who are joggled into a position where the easiest and most advantageous thing is to make a career out of being subject to them. The others, which is how I guess most people who'd want to read this would class themselves (as I would), correspondingly see themselves as Not Like That. We polarise into Daleks and

Radicals, or (say) Ofsted inspectors and coal-face workers. We blunder at every step into mutually exclusive passageways, constrictions of being which I have called Orthodoxy and the cacophony of dissent. We need, then, to step back from the temptations of polarity, to cultivate an abeyance in the midst of urgent calls to characterisation – because, paradoxically, such calls blot out encounter.

If such a litany entails anything at all it is that a 'refusal to encounter' needs irradiating with as many searchlights as possible. My own contribution to this is, in the end, only a battery of metaphors. But I do believe they are much more likely to be conductive and suffused with reality than the kind of programmatic exchange of sign-language which could so easily substitute for them. If we don't want to be confined to the 'suburb of dissent', we have to speak with as much unremitting faith in encounter as is available: metaphors may help us to do this because they don't encourage finalising[5], and so are not easily marginalised. They are capable of sustaining the Conversation.

Schools

5. Education encourages us to over-state things.

If you think I exaggerate in what follows – tough. For teaching is a decidedly exaggerated profession, and the world of teaching, though narrow from some points of view, distends magically once you're inside it. Other narrow worlds do so, too, but teaching more than many because it is that oxymoronic thing, a job whose subject and material is people, at the same time collaborative and adversary. In this curious situation, it might almost be said that you have to exaggerate in order to state. In fact, I think I'll exaggerate now. You *do* have to exaggerate in order to state.

Exaggeration in the world of teaching is a rich field. Teachers talk in exaggerated ways about themselves and their work; others talk in exaggerated ways about teachers and schools. The little world of education receives an incessant rain of comment, advice, interpretation, disparagement, praise, rumour, research, gossip, headline, documentation, feedback and publicity: MPs, parliamentary special advisers, quangos, councillors, counsellors, journalists, academics, businessmen, management consultants, social scientists, social workers, lobbyists, pressure groups, clerics, librarians, policemen and of course teachers, parents and pupils contribute to the inundation.

What I find teasingly obscure, and hence tending to make for an incalculable amount of distortion, is the provenance of this uneven deluge. What interests are being served, what warfare disguised, what consciences assuaged, what damage and hurt are being indulged and expressed? What varieties of motivation, misunderstanding, anxiety and vengefulness are fed and enriched by it?

None of us can say, of course. But this is not at all a limiting factor. It is, instead, a powerful incentive for it to be continued. Nothing can be proven – therefore everything can be said. Voices may be heard within this waterfall of sound which strive to overcome it, but it is in the nature of the problem that they are much more likely to strive for individual patches of sanity than that a lasting and trustworthy understanding should be found. And the very idea of an individual patch of sanity is not that far from an oxymoron itself.

Do we exaggerate the very importance of education under the law and inside institutions? In my secondary school we are (theoretically) in touch with Britain's future five hours a day, one hundred and eighty days a year, for five years out of their projected seventy. How important are we really going to be to their lives? - The answer, oddly if you don't think education is subject to inflation and distortion, is: more than you'd like to think. Teachers from Mr Chips to Julius Streicher have assumed enormous, and more than symbolic, importance in the minds of those committed to them. They may not listen to us, but they do remember us, as magnified examples of some of the ways it is possible to be an adult. (This is an argument for having a wide variety of types of people on your staff, if you are a headteacher.) The teacher who reduced you to tears, or whom you reduced to tears, or who talked about his family, or directed you in a musical, or had a famous bellow, or did conjuring tricks, or drove a comedy car, or never smiled or grinned like a demon, all these people are fixed in the theatre of memory. You recognise them at the dentist's twenty years later, or you read about them in the Crown Court details of your local paper.

We exaggerate our importance in the scheme of things, and are exaggerated, in a rather different sense, by our fellows (to summarise the last paragraph). Possibly as a consequence of this, we are capable of stylising ourselves in an effort to redeem our individuality (like Geoffrey Mabbott) from the surfeit of normativeness we engage with. We can behave to ourselves and others in stylised and exaggerated ways, overdone or underdone and occasionally grotesque. At times of crisis we are prone to make monsters of ourselves, to see others as monstrous, or to fight monstrously for the non-monstrous. Charges of infidelity or heresy can be brought with a breathtaking insouciance that recalls Dominican friars nosing out witches. All of us have heard some staffroom voice describe another as mad, sinister, treacherous, and that voice usually comes from somewhere experiencing quite a lot of discomfort of its own. But because judgments about people are what we work with, judgments about people are an instinctive recourse. I feel they're particularly prone to be made at times of great insecurity, and I'm certain they're habit-forming, bring only short-term relief, and as I said at the start, lead only to reduplication.

Other factors, other perspectives, bear on this, but I think they tend to the same conclusion. Nothing is irrelevant in teaching. We are a seismograph for the society we are part of. Crisis makes for instinctive recourses which make for caricature, impotence, and fragmentation.

6. Education is dramatic.

I do not want to be thought to be claiming that such things are continuously visible. Most teachers I have ever known love the profession, even if they are not the kind of people who proclaim such love stridently. They love it not because they are idealists or supremely gifted or have some mystical insight into young people that non-initiates don't have, but because they have grown up thinking of themselves as teachers, have worked their way into its atmosphere, which can be sustaining, and because its techniques, argot, camaraderie and above all its highly dramatic and personal nature have created a world for them into which their finances, marriages, friendships, habits, interests and characteristics are woven. It is because of this that when it goes wrong very selves are injured, and because of this that anxieties and recourses generated by the world outside are magnified and assume exaggerated forms. (Education, then, is a lens as well as a seismograph.)

Some of those other relevant factors now follow. They're all connected to exaggeration. Firstly, although we haven't the time to be conscious of it very often, our work continually exhibits bewildering changes of scale, its axes expanding and contracting wildly. We receive messages – calls upon us – of apparent tininess and of contrastingly Brobdingnagian proportions at the same instant. A look from a pupil in a crowded corridor as we try to focus on a Government initiative, perhaps. And although I'm not saying it's a frightfully disorientating factor it does foster a kind of uncertainty of perspective and priority. We are at every moment questers on a national enterprise and monitors of fleeting incident. The state of England and the state of our classroom are reflected in each other. The Chinese sage Mencius, giving the Duke of Chou the best parting advice he could think of, said "Do the great things as though they were small, and the small things as though they were great". I find this beautiful, and in some circumstances exciting, but what exactly is great or small in teaching (or life)? Is listening to two sides of a quarrel a great or small thing? Preparing for an interview? Questions of scale and perspective are notoriously confusing. However great the reach of the English language, however practised and logical our ability to think in hypothesis, and however innately sensitive our sympathies, they cannot solve this problem, precisely because they are designed *only to cope with it* and render us at least active, practical and effective in the face of it. The Conversation is not an exactitude-producing machine, not an algorithm, that is, however instantly plausible such an analogy may seem. As teachers these changes of scale, these perspective shifts, are part of our daily experience. They are also encouragements to exaggeration, because our reach, logic and sensitivity are distorted or diminished by insecurity. If we try to switch them on at moments when we're not capable of doing so, or if we try to protect them from the harm that the uncertainties of perspective can bring, we can leap prematurely into perspective-begotten shocks: my anger may not match your sense of your behaviour, your hurt may be invisible to my momentarily long view. The fact that your state of mind and preoccupation may be startlingly disconsonant with my own in our attempt to encounter each other is peculiarly dramatised in teaching. This brings me to the second factor. I once saw the playwright Edward Bond, seemingly inattentive, fashioning a paper aeroplane as he was earnestly asked to 'define' Drama. He made no answer, but floated the thing across the room, and, of course, he being famous, each avid eye followed it, and there was a quivering pause. Then it fell. *"That's Drama"*, he said, and we woke up. Is this the witchery of a very good performer, a very secure famous man faced by people who have paid to talk to him? I think not. The concentration and freedom of that moment have stayed with me. To me, at least, it means or is capable of meaning that 'Drama' is a series of intensely-observed frames or settings, in which almost anything can happen, and such is our hunger for illustrative meaning that at our best we meet the moment and take from its unfinalised capacity that which touches our own. We extend towards it and allow it room to populate us, or add to our population.

I think the whole concept of teaching is like that. One outcome of that intense concentration, scrutiny, and interpretation is that frames and settings seem to constitute its very nature. (Exam results? Depends how you look at them.) Some illustrations follow, but at this point it needs saying that this open-ended possibility and this consciousness of intense, almost obsessive, observation is *what it is like to be a teacher*. In some situations this is wonderfully exciting – with a class who haven't quite mastered an idea, but are hesitantly chasing it; with an understanding colleague or headteacher who needs you to open an occasion up to possibility, and who trusts you, and whom you trust. In others it just doesn't work. These frames and this observation are calls upon you, in the sense I mentioned earlier, and it is just as likely, or even likely, that either you or your interlocutor or both are at that moment not capable of Conversation. The moment may be vitiated by what passes for Politics, for example, and a deeply, but not very deeply, comforting urge to certainty, premature Judgment, a spurious and dishonest posturing, may result. This would be dramatic, as in those wonderfully exciting counterexamples, but it would not be successfully so, in the terms in which I interpret Edward Bond. A split between the you pretending to perform, the Geoffrey Mabbott in you, and the fugitive you that isn't currently able to perform would open up, and the heat generated by instability, exaggeration and the existence of frames and settings would flow in. And out: caricatures of oneself and others would take the place of a conductive reality.

7. The theatre of school induces a panic of interpretation.

It is difficult to realise quite how many such performative and dramatic occasions there are in teaching, just as it is to realise how many sales pitches we can be subject to each day. (Two thousand, I believe.) Twenty-five pairs of eyes watch you, or don't watch you, each lesson, anything up to forty pairs if you happen to work in a primary school. Hundreds can meet you in a short trip down the corridor at breaktime. Potentially thirteen hundred parents can phone me every day. Add to this fifty staff, a dozen governors, cleaners, classroom assistants, inspectors, peripatetic music teachers, maintenance men, grandparents, liaison teachers from other schools and colleges, county hall contacts, glaziers (we see a lot of glaziers), educational theatre luvvies, and people who simply seem to have popped in from the street for a bit of a chat, and it sometimes feels as though entire postal districts only have eyes for you. Each encounter is rife with possibility, unknownness, and the need for an adequate response.

All this human encounterability is the source of much of the buzz of teaching, and explains much of the pleasure and interest we gain from it. But it remains both problematic and a continually renewed fount of emotional distortion and defensiveness. Much repression or neutering of this open-ended unknownness is necessary simply to orient your attention, or we would, as George Eliot said, die of the *"roar on the other side of silence"*. The trouble is that we can't really rank these appeals for recognition fairly, and so we don't know, much of the time, how much real encounter we are editing out. This was brought home to me fairly recently when I was talking to a year 9 girl about her report. She's quiet, works amicably and productively, and is entirely free of the desperate self-advertisement which some pupils display. At the end of our chat, she picked up her bag and said, *"That's the first time you've spoken to me this year"*. I had, then, written a whole report on her abilities and current progress, and discussed it with her for a quarter of an hour, without realising that she'd been edited out. If she hadn't been capable of a good deal of detached patience and serenity, she'd have quite possibly felt the need to break out of the invisibility with which I'd cloaked her, and that can be, again, an opportunity for much emotional distortion and distension. A close friend of mine did, as it happens, find out how quickly patient serenity can turn to fury when he, too, was discussing a report with a quiet and undemanding pupil with whom he'd always seemed to have a peaceful understanding. He had written, *"Her only fault is a tendency to write **ad nauseam**."* She asked what it meant, and he gave her a dictionary; a moment's silence, then a shriek: *"So I make you **sick**, do I?"* She then gave him a passionate summary of his character, appearance, and parentage, and left.

There it is: an intensely-observed frame in which almost anything can happen. What can we *do* when the frame delivers such an unexpected picture? We can realise that such are the effects of framing, and try to discount or repair them; we can turn them into compensatory folklore ('over-emotional'); or we can defensively assert that we will never let the concentration and freedom of the frame put us in so vulnerable a position.

The last option was one chosen by a particular head of department from my probationary year. How I used to be impressed by the certainty with which he categorised instantly as sheep or goat *any* material, directive, proposition, circular or plan which came to his notice; teachers and pupils also. The overplus of calls upon him, the insistent performativeness of teaching, and probably the example of other, successful, people who did exactly the same, conspired to make him a producer, as well as consumer, of caricature. But he wasn't a bad teacher, or an uninteresting man. Because of that his own example, for a newly-qualified subordinate , was difficult to withstand, and what his example said to me was that resistance to the frame was part of being a teacher. What counted was to limit the number of framing opportunities and control the ones you couldn't avoid, perhaps by getting your framing in first: sheeping and goating is one way of doing this. His example takes us into the topic of survivalism through lessons taught in the staffroom.

Perspective, theatricality and exaggeration together create a habitat which is, to say the least, emotionally unsteady. New entrants to the profession do not always know how to navigate these choppy waters – it is quite possible for them to encounter some emotions, like hatred, for the first time in their lives. If such a thing happens, it is very reassuring to plunge into what we might call the recuperative folklore of the staffroom or to feel that at least, say, in the Modern Languages stock cupboard the airwaves defuzz and normality resumes.

This staffroom folklore is an interesting ingredient of school life. Every school, like every other serious and long-lasting assembly, has a hoard of stories both comic and tragic which seem to serve a purpose beyond mere amusement. The knowledge and relating of them may even be part of the unofficial induction process, the rite of passage, of new teachers. In them we are told that what we learned in college and what management are currently promoting are not the truth; that the reality of teaching is far stranger than appears from policy, interview or lecture. Just as children are told stories of plucky or resourceful youngest brothers or neglected kitchenmaids or ugly ducklings or giant killers, stories which in many cases are thousands of years old and in which the baroque horrors of cannibalism, dismemberment and madness are emphatically not mitigated, so teachers learn tales of revenge, deceit, malice and catastrophe. In both cases the hero is the same: the resourceful youngest child of the woodcutter, the young teacher who is skilled at survival. They teach us that though dangers exist where the pilot-books show nothing, survivalism, toughness and a kind of interested wariness will carry one past them. Every staffroom has its Brothers Grimm and its Ole Bill.

But it is easy to forget, while recounting school lore, that the anecdotes are themselves defensive, exaggerated and therefore 'instinctive recourses' which don't answer the truth of other people. They may foster survival, but they are actually complementary to the official versions of education which we hear at party conferences or read in inspection reports. Here is another polarisation. Staffroom folklore and inspection report are secretly cousins, both deviations from something that isn't fully there – encounter, Conversation, a matured openness. Stories of educated adults devoting years of thought and ingenuity to the scuppering of a rival, or of the head who only appoints the born-again to senior positions and whose management meetings feature (and, for all I know, consist of) the five of them on their knees praying for guidance and cleansing, or the friend and former teacher I came across last week leaving his Tesco visit until midnight to avoid any possible encounter with ex-colleagues, stories such as these are reciprocally related to the gleaming, desolate visions of Ofsted, the DfE, the QCA. They both nurture a premature extremity of judgment and an anxiety-driven belief in its adequacy. Because of them it is easier than it otherwise would be to make the rash and unevidenced assumption that one has somehow solved the truth of another person by calling him, or her, 'power mad' or 'a natural victim', or the truth of a lesson by calling it 'good' or 'unsatisfactory', or the truth of a school by calling it 'failing'. This very ease and swift, spurious clarity help sponsor belief in the value of 'extremity of judgment'.

The pursuit of a certainty like that is more than dangerous, given what I have said about exaggeration, perspective, performance, and recuperative folklore. Sheep, goats and caricatures are all creatures of the kind of insecure certainty which tends to get stuck fast in choosing one or other polarity. Certainty of that kind ends in impoverishment [6]. The magisterial and minatory certainties with which Dr Johnson, for instance, is often credited are an aggression *against* an intractable reality. Johnson actually spent his life writing and speaking *against* such aggressive certainty, not least because he was well aware of his own temptation to indulge it. But he entertained the notion to study and discredit it, and the unfinalised hope which his writings offer us is the product of his struggle against it.

8. Millennial insecurity increases teachers' urge to certainty.

So the pursuit of certainty is clearly at some level an attractive option. It is economical of mental effort, and requires less patience and less of what I can only call a kind of responsible passiveness than does openness to encounter and to the Conversation. Nevertheless, despite its allure, there are many occasions where it is quite patent that things in education are not as capable of satisfying resolution, of finality and certainty, as we are egged on by our anxieties to imagine that they should be.

In education, vexed questions are the norm. Questions that were once vexed remain vexed; they may be superseded for a while but they aren't resolved. I have yet to hear of a 'debate' within education that doesn't have a long history or does have an agreed outcome. Ideal position is set against ideal position: inclusion and special schools, skills and knowledge, public exams and continuous assessment, the whole person and the job market – I could go on but the list is so plonkingly tedious I can feel my brain scrabbling in the corners of my skull for a way out. The strange thing is that these are precisely the kind of questions which people often think they should sort out, once and for all. Probably they can't be decided, and it might be that only an over-anxious desire for completeness of mind would wish them to be. To anyone who has been teaching for twenty years or so they can begin to look like equally supportable dead ends. For at least a generation students and teachers have felt themselves expected to mature their views on such 'issues in education': what would be much more mature and reasonable, however, would be to think about how we can accept our rich, flexible, sensitive *lack* of certainty and keep it in good order for the enormous task of helping children come to know what learning is like.

Another weary standby on teaching courses since the 1970s has been the status of teaching as an occupation: Is Teaching a Profession? This too feels like a continuing neural itch working away through the years. Perhaps more clearly than the 'issues' described above, it betrays the potentially destructive effects of having to live with and in the ineradicable uncertainty of teaching. I have heard it said more than once that "the biggest mistake we made" was not to become part of the Civil Service in, I think, 1932. This might well have protected pay levels and stopped us from being the 'enemy within' in the 1980s, but (without researching it) I feel a likely reason it was turned down is that teachers were frantic to achieve their own professional identity, which might have been smothered in the ambiguous embrace of the Civil Service. Whether this is true or not, sensitive ambiguities like this will always be a focus of times of dissent or uncertainty because, as R H Thouless pointed out, the fact that an issue is controversial doesn't make people unsure about what to believe, but increases the conviction with which they believe whatever they do believe. The 'vexed questions' and the uncertain status of teachers seem at such times to demand answers with increased urgency, and the result is that we are less likely to bear with uncertainty and so invest more in the conviction which we happen to claim.

The hurt logic which is heard at such times can go like this: *"We're supposed to be public sector, and the only definition of 'public sector' is 'protected from market forces'. If they want me to be dedicated, they'd better protect me; if they want me to be exposed to the market-place then I'm in it for what I can get and they can't expect me to regard it as a vocation."* [7]

Strictly, this hurt logic is pretty unassailable, given its premises, although the Third Way is an as yet unfamiliar attempt *not* to give anybody those premises. However, what I want to point out here is the readiness with which times of anxiety suck us into one of two opposing havens – public sector or market forces, this side of a vexed question or that, sheep or goats. All are premature or defensive certainties, and perhaps they're all the more confidently expressed the less they're really believed in. The sucking-in process is most clearly felt when some urgent situation makes it sensible – a parent denying the school's right to administer its own rules in a voice like that of Ian Paisley with pre-menstrual tension, for instance, or being told we don't have a 'culture of success', or a story of abuse in the papers or a team of management consultants being downloaded on to an LEA. At times like this the havens start sucking, the folklore of the staffroom exercises its comforting mystery, the unions begin twitching and trying to establish positions of difference from each other, and a few teachers go sick, or crumble into 'not the person I married' or leave and start supply agencies. Then the caricatures are most seemingly real and the certainties at their most hospitable.

So questions like those leave me cold, because they are so palpably safety-manoeuvres. What is wrong in the world of education is not anything that could be solved with a wondrous *device* like new status, the right policies or proper funding, much as I too would like and enjoy them; what is wrong is a quality of human relationship which the millennial west is slowly forcing upon us. The question of status is a distraction. Like many other ambiguities in education, it is the wrong target, and we don't win anything for hitting it. We ought not, perhaps, choose our targets so easily. But the working and therefore personal life of a teacher is so constantly spinning and twisting to face this way and that as calls are made upon us and appeals made to us, and the faces and images which meet us as we make a new alignment are so existentially various that we can seem to present a different I at each turning. Kim's question - *"Who is Kim?"* [8] - is asked of the wondering teacher many times in a working life, and the urgent need to answer it is never dimmed: if it feels dimmed, that is only one kind of answer.

Perhaps this is no more than to say that the living with an uncertainty which reaches deep into one's being is a requirement, possibly the major requirement, of the kind of person who will make a happy and various teacher. I don't mean we ought to think too badly of ourselves if we fall away many times from that requirement; only that we shouldn't forget it. There is nothing wrong with a teacher who at times blows his top, or fails to respond to a call, or assesses a situation badly. That is after all part of our variety – we have a right to be wrong, as well as a duty to be uncertain. We too must be allowed to be various as we hope to respond adequately to the variety in each of our charges. The kind of thing which can destroy this capacity is not having poor status, the wrong policies or inadequate funding, but the slow encouragement to think of everything to do with education in terms of a poisonous certainty [9].

Consequently, it isn't all that much of a surprise to us if we are more ready than we should be to relate to each other with caricatured and defensive certainty. Continually to jack ourselves up to a properly adequate sense of our own responsibility (which is different from accountability), to bear continually in mind the temptation for others to see us only in our edited or performing versions, to have to unite in ourselves a huge capability, a provisionally coherent sense of what we, and all other voices in education, are up to, to bring all of this to each unpredictable moment without spilling it, *and* continually to surround it with the disparate vitalities of our personal existence, is an enormous and a consuming task. What can it feel like? A tight, enclosed space, at the point of bursting, of repletion rather than completion; a hollow overinflated, filled to its reach, bloated, unable to contain a content which is eruptive and constantly regenerating, an enormous massing of forces whose nature is solely to press further against their bounds: that, I would guess, or something like it, is a recognisable sensation to many of us these days, and perhaps one which the emotions we invested in the Millennium were unconsciously meant to assuage.

9. 'School X' displays all these millennial ills.

So we come to the consideration of a school in which a lot of these themes are rehearsed both comically and tragically. It isn't typical, - or is it? – but its distinctiveness gives us a distance from it which allows it to be used to illustrate some of them. It also isn't by any means a 'failing school', I ought to say; 'failing schools' or schools which might become so are often much more human, optimistic and successful places.

This establishment, which I'll call 'School X' because of its pleasing air of the cloak-and-dagger, is or was a smallish comprehensive which achieved results not far short of the national average and had gained over the years a reasonably secure reputation. The staff were composed mainly of locally born and educated men and women with a sprinkling, rare for the county, of on the whole more highly-qualified subject specialists from other parts of Britain. Several older teachers remained from the Girls' Grammar which had been absorbed into its structure and which provided the buildings for its top-heavy sixth form. It had a sense of its own history – photographs of staff from the 1920s, all grave, bearded and archaic enlivened the entrance hall, along with puzzling items of defunct ironmongery in glass cases: 'A' level Art? Debris from a gas-main explosion? Rose gardens, a theatre, home-made sausage rolls in the canteen and a school cat, itself rather grave and responsible-looking, added to the image which met the visitor.

Needless to say, the reality was much more complex. It has always seemed strange to me that one school of fifty teachers can differ quite so much, not in its 'systems' or results as in its ethos, its existential character, what it is like to be a member of it, from another, nearby and technically similar school. The answer must lie in their histories and the extent to which they have been moulded by 'leadership', that magic word. Influential and impressive as are the abilities of headteachers to think on their feet and come up with operational solutions, new initiatives or new funding, more influential still, because of its primitive exemplary nature, is the emotional character of the head, which is magnified by and active upon the wholeness of the school. In School X, the head had created a remarkable blend of anxiety, dishonesty, and aggression which made it for many teachers an almost impossible place to work in.

Two-thirds of the staff had been there a very long time; turnover among the rest was extremely fast. There were signs of recently-vanished, short-lived careers everywhere: abandoned lockers bearing strange names, faces appearing on one staff photograph and disappearing from the next, bits of personal bric-a-brac discovered in stock cupboards like dinner plates on the Marie Celeste. The hard core of the staff were so closely interwoven, being each others' sisters, cousins, husbands, ex-lovers and current lovers, that one had to develop an anthropologist's sensitivity to their relationships. When I came to work there, this was one of the first survival tips offered to me, by a young teacher who had taken to wearing concealed recording equipment, given to her by her policeman husband, for chats with senior management. Tips, hints and asides were a great feature of life at School X: how to leave the premises without passing the head's office, which genial and approachable figures not to go anywhere near, and of course the importance of using four pins for a staffroom notice rather than one. There were also whispered stories of long-term illnesses, sudden resignations, and long inveterate campaigns of sedate victimisation.

As what now seems a natural extension of this, a fervid atmosphere of betrayal and everyday treachery prevailed. I can see now the eagerness with which one figure pranced off to the head to point out that two history teachers were chatting during exam invigilation. New senior tutors were treated to an exhibition of breathless paranoia where they were repeatedly told that now they were *"the boss's men"*, and encouraged to resign if they found this difficult. The head of English had achieved her position in a palace *coup* unprecedented in my experience, whereby she and her deputy had provided unofficial weekly reports on the inefficiency of her predecessor, resulting in his headlong demotion over the summer – *"have a good holiday, Jenkins, I've got some bad news when you get back"* – and accounting for his silence and isolation in the staffroom. Even, or especially, the pupils were encouraged to behave like this. Deputations were regularly seen handing in petitions of complaint. In no case did these amount to nothing: the chap in charge of computers received an official written warning resting on nothing more substantial than his breezy informality with students, and a teacher of English the same because the eighty-odd texts she'd recommended for supplementary 'wider reading' didn't come with detailed synopses. The worst of these cases involved an inoffensive Art teacher who resigned on health grounds after a well-orchestrated hit by year 11 pupils. During registration, one of them climbed on his desk, clasped his face and belched richly into it. Automatically, he moved the boy away by perhaps six inches, pushing his arm with the flat of his hand. This was deemed to be an assault, and he was suspended that afternoon.

In this atmosphere honesty collapsed. Conversation in the staffroom was severely constrained; several teachers began to use it as a means of publicising their own lack of vulnerability, their aggressions and certainties. Holes and corners developed for the production of gossip. At least twice teachers were arraigned for having been overheard being 'negative'. One teacher told me, and

I recognised the symptoms, that it became difficult to know what you really did think – your reactions were deformed by the encroachment of a quasi-Stalinist orthodoxy. For the first time it made me think that the knowledge of truth is something that can be withered, that its possibility is a consequence of the spirit in which we meet each other, not something purely self-grown, and that only an openness to the unknown, a kind of natural courage by which we let those we meet remain themselves, that is, remain radically unknown, can foster it.

This is one of the things I meant by writing that the world of teaching 'distends magically once you're in it'. Although School X wasn't a gulag, serious harm to that openness could be done there as well as in a gulag – one of the conveniences of truth is that it can be learnt in devastating, or merely irritating, classes. Truth's possibility can be threatened, images can be swollen, the influence of leadership can be magnified inside such classes.

It may have taken the head of School X fifteen years or more to create this atmosphere. It will take a lot more than fifteen years to reverse it, because once it has taken hold an atmosphere is a very tenacious creature. Staff who can't adapt to it leave, with or without damage; staff who remain are deformed by surviving, or blossom into their own imitative paranoiac mock-stability. I think the fundamental 'emotional characteristic' of this head was a desire for absolute and systematic watertightness, for a disturbing completeness which is the contrary of 'openness' and 'unknownness', and it was that which formed, over the years, School X's atmosphere. This fostered both many acts of asinine splendour and a kind of enacted theatricality which seeped into every activity. Banning sixth-formers and teachers from saying "Hi" or "Hello" to each other, proposing uniforms for the staff, and standardising the value of leaving presents according to status and service (the week this was adopted, the head announced his own retirement) are all evidence of this niggling desire for completeness. So was remodelling the school entrance to protect his 'study' by a tortuous system of interlocking defiles, offices, a shredding room and a sort of double-locked scullery of his own.

The theatricality was seen most clearly in staff meetings which took place, neatly enough, in the theatre, unlike the Christmas gathering in the staffroom where the head gave his Joke its annual outing from the mortuary. A long table with plants and carafes on it stood in front of the proscenium. Here sat the head, three deputies and an extraordinary individual called the Head of Studies, who walked ramrod-straight with tiny bouncing buttock-clenching footsteps, spoke in a fast arrhythmic staccato and played Squealer to the head's Napoleon. They entered in procession, with a dramatic pause before the head, who must have peeped through the curtains, came slowly, undeviatingly, into view. Seating arrangements for the rest of the staff were semiotically interesting. Eager customers sat centrally at the front. The favoured seats, for which much comically unacknowledged competition took place, were neither right in the head's eye at the front (though as the seats were raised in tiers we were all in his sight) nor too far back, which would be equivalent to holding up a sign saying 'worried'. In the main, the departments sat together – English and Maths centrally, and departments like Textiles, clearly not central, at the sides. A few mavericks or terminal patients like the ex-head of English sat with gaps between them and the body of the congregation. Now prepared speeches were made. 'Agenda items' were 'spoken to'. They referred to things like 'clients' (ie parents), 'educational plants' (ie schools) and 'performance indicators' (for instance, being unavoidably late to a lesson). Unsurprisingly, the majority preserved a diverse silence. Some of us couldn't perform the lingo without laughing or gagging. Some sat frozen waiting for release. Some simply couldn't think of any acceptable contribution. The noises-off of other staff meetings at other schools didn't happen – people apologising for being late, the hiss of the tea-urn, polite or impolite interruptions, whispered comments, a brief gale of laughter. Nor was there any chatting as we left. Nor were *any* objections raised to *any* proposal from the head in the time I spent there. Atmosphere produced a spurious unanimity.

Each performance of a staff meeting was, therefore, logically perfect. I came to believe the head needed such regular fixes of perfection, like his watertight systems, much more than would be simply explained by efficiency. Instead, they assuaged his anxiety. Their extravagance and their nigglingness bear witness to a desire to avoid the unpredictable and the various. They are expressions, far-fetched admittedly, of a radically insecure sense of self. In them we can sense a tinkering or interference with the inner and outer worlds, the creation of a system which the head's self can fully inhabit and which mirrors him in a sense autistically, and the deformation of other selves to accord with it. The result is a crazed alignment whereby anxiety is assuaged and at the same time insecurity powerfully indulged.

10. A 'rogue subjectivity' infests places like School X.

Enough has been said about this school to indicate that exaggeration, defensive certainty, the collapse of difference and honesty, and a deep urge for perfection formed its atmosphere or style. These things are to some extent self-replicating. They may not be all-powerful – after all, though I haven't described them, decent people did manage to survive there – but they certainly influenced the way in which teachers there felt themselves to be teachers, and the ways in which they related to each other. Although the head of School X would say (amongst other things), were he to read this and recognise himself, that they produced the goods, it depends which goods you mean. Exam results wouldn't have been materially altered by a less neurotic ethos, and the edited-out children, who couldn't contribute to the league tables, might have learned something more than obedience. I suspect the extravagance of this system was neurotic, and that its function was purely to be exercised , to engage in idealised struggle against difference, and to be the expression of a kind of rogue subjectivity entirely blind to the liberty and variety of other ways of being. And that means it is blind to education itself.

Why have I written so much of School X? There are at least two reasons. In the first place, it began to set me thinking of the defensiveness not only of those who felt themselves denied (like the Art teacher) but of those who did the denying. And in the second place, although as I said it can't be called a typical school, I do believe it is a highly revealing one. Precisely because it isn't typical, it is illustrative. Conditions of normality don't display the effects of underlying tensions as clearly as conditions of extremity. What it illustrates is the effects of treating the school purely as an assembly of reflective surfaces: *image* was, in the end, the 'goods' it produced. I believe that is worth noticing, not simply because of the damage it inflicts on human lives, nor simply because of the sheer wastage of talent and man-hours it makes necessary, but because it is a frivolous distortion of the possibility of truth in education. In a sense, I'm not writing as a teacher at all here, but wholly about the contrast between the shadowiness and unreality of the production of images and the sudden reeking richness, the *impact*, of granting each other a finally unknowable liberty and reality.

Magic

11. Emotion-and-rigour.

There seems to be an assumption, floating somewhere over England, though not often, as far as I know, deeply experienced by any real individual, that as we breast the year 2000 we have attained a gratifying maturity and realism, a heartening sense of really being at home with ourselves. I shall be discussing this fantasy via some of its metaphors later; for now, I want to confine discussion to just two of its more seemingly reasonable aspects. These are that we are wise and de-centred enough to organise our affairs with scientific rigour and not to put up with any more childish illusions or class-war-inspired social myths; and that we are at ease enough with our Susie Orbach-sponsored emotions to happily accept the riskiness of being properly open, sincere and grown-up [10]. At first sight these might appear radically different, though both to do with grown-upness: what, after all, could be more distinct than rigour and emotion? It's true that anyone encountered in, say, a pub actually espousing these beliefs as such would be considered slightly off their head; the oddity is, though, that this doesn't diminish their entire acceptability as part of our political consciousness. It may be what we substitute for national debate. Perhaps it is less that people cling personally to these beliefs, and more that there is a kind of exhausted acquiescence in them: they seem to do us little harm.

I think their apparent divergence, like their seeming general acceptance, is actually an illusion. There is after all a kind of satisfactoriness, as if all eventualities have been covered, in the union of science and feeling, rigour and emotion – remember 'neurotic completion'. The comfort they offer is that we have overcome the appalling conflicts, the Kantian antinomies, of the past. The Millennium is the symbol of this, and, I should say, the political vacuum of the last fifteen years the efficient cause. A final cause is more difficult to prise out, but the dislocating effects of the new technologies, with their roots in the nineteenth century, are an inviting candidate.

This impinges on us in the educational world in too many ways to count; but it seems safe to say that we are supposed to be *emotionally committed and open* about our work, and also to be keen to be judged by *rigorous*, indeed *scientific, measurement*. These twin mottoes are to be trumpeted loudly into the public vacancy. And they make themselves felt wherever we look in and around our work. If we take, for instance, the mission statement and the Ofsted judgment, I think they are rather more legible than usual if read in the light of what I have said above. I choose these two items for comment because they show public language at one kind of extreme. They work hard to enact themselves, they are highly visible and 'accessible', they stand guard over education like Gog and Magog, and they are, I think, deeply fraudulent. To anticipate, the mission statement treats an *object* or a construct like a school as if it were a *subject*, and the Ofsted judgment treats a *subject*, like a teacher, as if it were an *object*. The first corresponds to emotionality, the second to rigour. Rather than being a necessary corrective to (mythical) woolly-liberal thinking, these are simple dislocations which can be explained by the pressure to brandish surfaces rather than participate in the Conversation; and their fundamental fault is that they severally take each half of human reality and make them stand, in turn, for the living and mutually penetrable duality which is the truth, put it however we prefer, of human experience.

12. The magic of the mission statement.

Let's see how they do it. The mission statement, in the first place, is surely a very anxious document. Moreover, it mimics a human voice, and in so doing it offers

81

a gratifying effect of simplicity, cutting through (in a very modern way) the disconcerting complexity of voices, points of view, and calls upon us which we noticed earlier.

In terms of anxiety, the mission statement is rather different from an old-fashioned statement of aims that might have appeared in a business plan or the preamble to a statute setting up a public service. Some such statements in the past have been little more than legal disclaimers limiting liability or defining one's territory. They may have been cast in brass on the walls of head office, or they may have been enunciated in a company report. Their importance was that they were stated *somewhere*, as for instance the *London Gazette*: we are all deemed legally to have been advised of anything that appears in the *London Gazette*. Today's mission statements are much more like *moral* disclaimers abjuring detachment: they are presumed evidence of the kind of corporate soul that is claimed; and rather than being content to repose on a brass plaque in a dusty corner, they are of their nature desperately seeking audience. They are above all highly emotional *claims* which one wishes to be judged by, rather in the manner of chivalric oaths or, to lower one's sights a little, the extravagant affidavits of childhood ("I hope I'm struck by lightning in the next minute if I'm lying!"). They are testaments to one's utter faithfulness, seriousness, reality and depth, and the fact that they are now standard kit for government departments, corporations, local authorities, hospitals, schools, charities, sports centres, supermarkets, and, any moment now, kebab shops, is surely a remarkable thing. They witness to an anxiety which is very revealing – the anxiety that they are not *believed in*. No admission of any desire to expand, maximise profit or activity, or simply continue would be – of course – permissible. Instead the mission statement is an increasingly vain attempt to raise the stakes, to *really* impact on reality, almost to bring into being the truth of what one is by an *act*, an act of will. That mimicry of the human voice represents a claim to subjectivity: that the institution, far from being cold, soulless or inhuman, is in fact *one of us*. It is listening, and it cares. And that is what is important, not what it actually *says*.

The emotional atmosphere attending this is so intense that, in principle, it would make no difference if, stuck for a really good mission statement, you downloaded one from a mission statement supplier. It's becoming harder to assume that adopting one's intimate blazon like this is insincere, or if insincere bad, because a vague conflation of performance with intent is – in principle – quite close. Strict but mere compliance with guidelines is felt to be not only OK but, strictly, all that is possible. We might call such an attitude an example of 'technolore', a subdivision of folklore appropriate to the cyberspace age.

One might refer this anxious act of will to an act of magic. Magical language, which simply by being uttered brings about a new state of affairs, is a very old fantasy, indeed so old we could almost term it natural. The anthropologist Bronislaw Malinowski traces this 'dynamic' function of language to childhood:

> "The child lives in a world of effective words. While to the adult words may in certain circumstances become real forces, to the child they normally are so. They give him an emotional hold on reality ... In all the child's experience, words, when seriously uttered, *mean* in so far as they act ... [The child has an] early magical attitude towards words, [an] infantile feeling that a name conjures up a person, that a noun sufficiently often repeated will materialise the thing ..." [11]

The act of will by which the mission statement brings together intention and performance, and the anxiety which drives it, are the very same thing as this infant's magic. An 'emotional hold on reality' is exactly what is conjured into existence, and it brings us neatly to the question of the mission statement's curious seductiveness.

The appealing simplicity, brevity, impact of the mission statement is the second of its attributes I should like to focus on. I don't feel I am at all insensible to the appeal of my own school mission statement ("School Y seeks to be a caring community, where pupils will achieve."). It pounces on us as we round corners, and as none of us, clearly, would be willing to disagree with it, we are reminded of ourselves when it does so. It almost feels like our name – 'School-Y-seeking-to-be-a-caring-community'– rather in the manner of the name of a Pequot Indian baby or a Welsh railway station. Other schools' and colleges' versions may be more anxiously ambitious, well decked with bullet points, aspirational logos, and website addresses, but ours does for us. I have no quarrel with this, its actual content. What I do have a quarrel with is its form, provenance, existence. I have a quarrel with the garbling discord of a national atmosphere which obliges us to gain strength from the simple and spurious sensation of brevity, of encapsulation in itself, and I have a further, if related, quarrel with its air of having cornered our essence. Encapsulation gives us something to *hold on to*, like the old Open University history programmes which flash up little decorative cartouches with 'Peace preceded Protestantism' in them. It presents itself as a talisman, something central, urgent, protected and generative. It is a verbal logo. Like "$E=mc^2$" it nabs a blindingly complex system of differences in the core of its nature and, cutting metaphysical corners, displays its heart. This is far too close for comfort to the magical function of language which Malinowski called attention to. Like the soundbite, the formula, the mantra (or even the *name*) it is a clue to an abiding need to be assured that all really is well, that somewhere truths are simple, that the dizzy phantasmagoria can be trusted, and that reality is, after all, manageable. I think this need supplies itself with superstitions, and as we have seen superstitions are not the most reliable guide to genuine experience, or into the Conversation.

13. The magic of Ofsted.

Like the mission statement, the Ofsted judgment is intensely a linguistic act, and though not a kind of anguished plea for recognition, it is just as self-validating and just as effective in its marshalling of contemporary superstitions.

I want to concentrate on the bit of it which is handed (or was, in the England of 1998) in a sealed envelope to the individual teacher. There are several characteristics of this document which I feel testify to a possibly misplaced respect for scientific and "objective" judgment, or rather are evidence of Ofsted's usage of such a respect, and each of them contributes to its prestige. The fact that one has literally no idea what judgments have been made until one opens the thing does little to diminish its mystique.

Firstly, the document itself is called a record of a *profile*. Not, that is, a judgment, which by contrast suddenly feels full of individual human content; judgements are unique and variable actions of a judge, but a *profile* is a simple representation. To be seen 'in profile' means to expose to view aspects of oneself which one cannot view oneself. It is, then, a record of one's perhaps more vulnerable parts. A profile of a figure may be its outline or boundaries, the extent to which it reaches, or the shape it casts in shadow. A profile of a person, like a mugshot, is produced automatically, without interest or interference, and without its subject being able to affect it. It is meant to be as close as rationally conceivable to the truth as it exists in itself, *sub specie aeternitatis*. It identifies one, and penetrates to one's heart; or rather, it does the opposite, remaining purely and coldly external, whilst excluding 'one's heart' as not capable of representation: as subjective. But it is meant to capture, and to seem to penetrate, one's reality. And it can be used against one.

The 'profile' reminds me rather of the way Sherlock Holmes' mind was supposed to work. Unlike other detectives, S H relied on nothing human whatsoever in his work (despite cocaine and Mendelssohn). Miss Marple solves crimes by finding their analogues in the village of St Mary Mead; Hercule Poirot by thinking like the murderer. Holmes, instead, by virtue of a prodigious relevant knowledge and a card-index system, allows facts to settle down and arrange themselves while he shoots bullets above the mantelpiece. In Holmes' world, the solution is logically already there in the problem; what he has to do is suppress the confusing appearance of difference between them. The Office for Standards in Education would like to be thought to be doing much the same thing.

Secondly, the structuring of the document is curious. The griff, the list of Xs that like your genetic code identifies your teacherliness absolutely, is centrally placed between, at the head, the rather unnecessary information that the paper shows 'a profile of the quality of teaching in the lessons seen taught by you', and at its foot a series of hedging disclaimers, no doubt legally necessary, about what may and may not be done with it. That is, its identity and its provenance seal in between them the profile itself, which appears therefore as a core or kernel, something central, ultimate and guarded. Five columns of modishly impressive codes, numbers and Xs make up this profile, the codes standing for subjects (in my case, incorrect in a puzzlingly random way). DR stands for 'Drama' and EN/DR presumably stands for 'Drama within English': why have the *words* been substituted? To make it look more abstract; to withdraw it a little further from the potentially subjective use of old-fashioned things like words. The Xs are the hits on the three columns headed 'Excellent or very good', 'Satisfactory or good' and 'Less than satisfactory'. Each X provides an appropriately focussed-looking symbol, like the cross-hairs in a rifle sight. Underneath, the number of Xs is neatly totalled, with a zero if there are no Xs in that column. Below that, on my copy, is a line of dashes with '9 lessons' at their centre. Nothing could be more objective, less distorted by comment or qualification, or more of a completed, symmetrical, permanent, computer-generated Record. I feel like writing 'Amen' at the end of it, which incidentally does something to show how close this kind of scientistic objectivity is to 'technolore'.

The comforts of tabulation such as this are fairly clear. It magically suppresses subjectivity. In strict accordance with the demands of scientism, it translates an immensely complex range of human unknownness into a neat diagram, or a formula [12]. The barefaced cheek with which it ignores the glaring facts that (a) 'inspectors', i.e. passive registers of reality – not 'judges', note – differ wildly from each other and (b) so do the procedures of teams of inspectors [13], is a clear bit of evidence for the seductive appeal of such diagrams. With such perverse glamour, the barefaced cheek doesn't need to be apologised for. As far as possible, everything to do with subjectivity (teacher, inspector, kind and degree of learning) has been transformed into object, externality.

Perhaps we could conclude that these features of the profile - its design, symbolism, and name - remove it, as far as possible, from language that is the product of a human mind, selected, written, responsible. It seeks, that is, to be reclassified as language that has effortlessly *arisen*, not as the result but as the simple expression of the antiseptic process of observation. This would collapse, as far as may be, the distance between infallible observation and humanly responsive language.

Such an effect is strikingly close to that of the mission statement (recall its conflation, or collapse, of performance and intent). Despite their apparently contrary treatment of subject and object, reversing them in different directions, this is able to happen because their manipulation of language - in effect, the spirit in which they conceive it - is in both cases *magical*. It is enacted, dynamic, performative, closes the risky gaps between intention and utterance (mission statement) and between observation and judgment (Ofsted profile), and, we must allow, is emotionally powerful. This power, to which none of us can be immune, perhaps derives from the intensity with which they mimic human calls upon us in a world where communication is suddenly problematic.

Part of the hypnotic compulsion they exert is due to the fact that they allow no appeal. The heated sincerity of the one and the chill gloss of the other are, for the moment, invulnerable, because the statement focuses hitherto formless attitudes in its brevity and bravura and the profile is detached from being judged because it claims to eschew judgment from the start. Evidence for this compulsion could be found in the fact that it is much easier not to criticise them than to attempt a critique; personally, I am aware of no such critique. They may be felt to be simply part of the way the modern world is, and so that exhausted acquiescence I cited above is seen here too [14]. And the fact that they apparently perform such extraordinary tricks with language may render the acquiescence the more docile.

This is a remarkably duff kind of scientism, and a remarkably anxious kind of emotionalism. I suggest that the fundamental trick they pull is to work with subjectivity and objectivity in isolation from each other.

Close-focus vignettes of this severance are the tempting harbours of *either* this extremity or that, the twin poles of scientism and Orbachian feeling, and the 'rogue subjectivity' that stalked School X. Perhaps we should begin to sense a kind of creeping solipsism, a madmanlike kind of sanity, in some of these effects, leaking towards us like warmth from the next room.

14. The roots of this magical defensiveness are in childhood.

I've been attempting to argue that (1) relationships, not only in education, between oneself and another self, oneself and others in the mass, and oneself and one's self-image, are responsive to shifts in the sand beneath us; that (2) one way of looking at this is to see those relationships stretched on a scale between acceptance of, and denial ('collapsing') of, risky gaps, differences and uncertainties; that (3) this denial can be seen in the erasures of gaps between intention and utterance, observation and judgment, or interpretation and certainty; that (4) our social living is *made* of such gaps; and that (5) closing them, e.g. by caricaturing another person or shoring up one's fragile sense of self with identity-supplements, is an essentially *magical* way of inoculating ourselves against the indeterminacy of the Conversation.

Furthermore, a symptom of this curious neo-magic (which I'm not competent to go into exhaustively, and which is in any case far too huge a topic to dwell on here) is that audacious cleavage of the Conversation into the giant opposing façades of Subject and Object. All I will say about this now is that it allows the magical attitude to present selfhood as merely subjective, and itself as the corresponding objective. Real, responsible, other-populated selfhood is killed off or bisected into, firstly, a visible, colourful, emotional, and powerless part termed 'subject', and, secondly, a hidden, security-conscious, manipulative part masquerading as 'object' (like a ceremonial figurehead and the power behind the throne). In this way of arranging matters, there is now no room for that which is truly not-ourselves but which inhabits us – for that which we have disguised under the name 'reality'.

More of that later. For now, I want to suggest that this magical attitude is a purely defensive system born of the fear-of-uncertainty. It brings to mind the defensive strategies unearthed by the psychologists, particularly Freud, under the title 'ego-defences'. The most radical of these is Regression.

Freud's reputation has suffered a good deal in recent decades, not least because he is easy to portray as the kind of Edwardian patriarch against whom rebellion is not only a pleasure but also a duty (a danger he foresaw). But one part of his oeuvre hasn't dated – his description of the many ways in which we can reduce, or evade, conflict. This, according to Freud, is first discovered by the new-born baby, whose strong feelings of protest at being deprived of the serene identity between itself and its surroundings which it knew before birth are never forgotten. Foetal existence is remembered as omnipotence. But when the developing child has to undergo learnings which involve loss – gradually discerning the boundaries of the ego, primarily (which we can relate to the acceptance of difference) – then anxiety, and even rage, are the result. Such learnings imply a variety of disconnections in the self, the opening of risky gaps between the ego and the world, and between the ego and what it makes of itself. What if the conflict, the split in itself, becomes too disturbing? Then we regress, in fantasy, to a previous state of being, which in our terms is to collapse differences. What is interesting here is that none of this power of refusal is ever utterly thrown away. Regression, and more specific defences associated with it (eg projection) are options to be carried through life. Admittedly, some of us may be more inclined to take advantage of it than others, but echoes of it may be heard in many places – in adult nostalgia, for instance (the horns of Elfland faintly blowing). When difficulties arise in the real world of adulthood, Freud says, there's a "tendency for the libido to return to pregenital cathexes", ie regress to previous attachments, and in order to do so we are thrown back upon defences we learned in the cradle.

So there is evidently a similarity of pattern between ego-defences and the intolerance of differentiation and distrust of gaps we looked at earlier. I want to make two more connections here – firstly, that between defences and constructiveness, and, secondly, that between defences and magic. The former is important because it should be made clear that, whilst what I have been pointing out may well be an implicit fracturing of Conversation, it is not always easy to see it as solely destructive. Big things can be created by it. Constructed systems of analysis and control and judgment may have as part of their motivation the protection they afford to the ego (even though it is a protection which doesn't finally satisfy the ego). I certainly do not mean to say, however, that this is their only motivation; simply that we do not know enough about them in today's fabulously complex world to trust them blindly. (Though it is, of course, easy to relapse into 'exhausted acquiescence'.)

Both connections may perhaps be made by considering the attractive case presented by the anthropologist Weston LaBarre for tracing the origins of magic and religion to the constructive effects of regression. For LaBarre, Shamanistic magic, which imagines human control over the spirit world, is an adult expression of a child's potentially violent reaction to recognising that the ego has boundaries (and so is schizophrenia – *"the schizophrenic is a foetus which is yet in the world"*). Religion and priestcraft he views as a double regression in the face of the demands of later stages of ego-development for the learning of discipline, conscience and identification with the father. So while material culture, to LaBarre, is an adaptation to the outer world, magic and religion are adaptations to the "unsolved problems and unmet needs" of the inner world, "narcissistic, impatient, intolerant of anxiety and ambiguity" [16].

There is a kind of ego-defence, then, which is emotionally powerful because of its infantile origin, which is 'intolerant of anxiety and ambiguity', which reacts instinctively when under threat, which in some circumstances will interpret emergence into a world less amenable to the ego as such a threat, and which may well be related to the universal appeal of magic. If we add to this that the very existence of other human beings who are essentially irresolvable and uncontrollable, not to say incapable of being utterly known, might well be evidence of such a world, and that a kind of radical uncertainty is a big thing to accept in one's character, then doesn't this sound familiar? And why should education, in the sense of being involved in other people's learning, with its similarly prehistoric roots in the family, be exempt from the anxieties that (for LaBarre) produced religion? Regression is active and even creative in our 'little world of education' just as elsewhere. The roots of our superstitious belief in the adequacy of the simple judgment of others, and the fear of gaps, lie here.

If this is true, it's not always immediately obvious. I think myself one reason for this [17] is the communicative complexity of today's world, which I tried to characterise earlier: the vast difference in status, intimacy, authority of the calls upon us and the calls we have to make. This might correspondingly mean a vast difference in status, intimacy and authority of the kinds and degree of emotional reaction we exert or have recourse to, and the kinds of places or situations these reactions emerge in. I mean that it need not be contradictory to find a given man or woman, pretty good at being an adult in some kinds of situation, feeling the faint stirrings of a kind of regression when they help perpetrate a mission statement, or find themselves in charge of a school full of rebarbative snags in the form of wily and experienced teachers, or simply by being a teacher having to cope with the sudden vanishing of things they thought they had known. Naturally, if such a person were so tempted, then hiding the truth of the matter from themselves as well as others would be essential: we have an interest, perhaps all of us, in disguising regressiveness.

Despite not being blazingly obvious, I think some such interpretation is almost necessary. We are tempted to some kinds of reaction because of the world beyond teaching, and because teaching magnifies some characteristics of that world; and such reactions are not, cannot be, purely private but emerge or erupt into institutional acts. The desires for certainty, completeness and the collapsing of difference are three of them.

But having said so much about one kind of defence, I do not want to lose sight of the fact that many others are perhaps even more visible – the difference is that, while regression may provide a clue to large-scale and seemingly impersonal effects (like systems of judging), others may be more clearly seen in individual people or moments. Perhaps they may be a muted or better-adapted version of regression, carried out not so much in the core as at the edges of personality.

I mean the kinds of defence mechanism which, following Freud's 1923 work *The Ego and the Id*, have been winkled out and refined by investigators influenced by him – Melanie Klein, for instance, or D W Winnicott. Extreme situations, but also ordinary' situations, have proved to be teeming with such things. Bruno Bettelheim's *The Informed Heart* observed a dozen of them in use in the Nazi concentration camps. Gordon Allport's *The Nature of Prejudice* lists the following as Jewish defences against racism in the America of the 1950s: obsessive concern, denial of membership, passivity, clowning, stronger in-group ties, cunning, self-hate, prejudice against black people, sympathy, militancy, enhanced striving, and neurosis [18] . Or in teachers' terms, one by one: I'm a stickler for detail, you know what teachers are like, I'll do it if it's in my contract, I'm the staffroom Will Hay (or Lenny Bruce), stick together, I'll out-manoeuvre him, I'm no good at this, bloody social workers, tell me all about it, call the union, I must do more, and Arrgh. Just as School X wasn't a gulag, yet a kind of mini-Stalinism walked abroad there, so this sort of thing isn't just alive in the ghettos or death-camps. It's natural, so natural that we could equally well compile another such list, starting with Nostalgia (it wasn't like this before Keith Joseph/continuous assessment/the abolition of caning - delete as appropriate). The more we list such defences the more clearly bells are rung in teachers' minds -overcompensation, for instance: "I love the children", or as a defence against the disquieting (to some) thought that none of us really knows how to characterise education: "The bottom line is we're running a business." Certainty and stridency are often compensations for the guilt one feels if one is not at ease with something - a radical uncertainty, for instance – and yet feels that one ought to be.

15. At some level, we are aware of all this, because we think of ourselves as lacking reality.

The strange habits and ecology of schools which I indicated above (and, believe me, these were tips of icebergs) were put down to fear of an 'unknowable liberty'; the magical language we then looked at seemed to be part of a sterile-conditions operation to rip apart 'subject' and 'object', followed by, for security reasons, their collapse into versions of each other. These pieces of spiritual jugglery were then likened to defensive manoeuvres associated with the classical Freudian defence of regression. Is it possible there was once a situation in which the relations of subject and object were not puzzled or deformed like this? Visions of some lost unity are very many, of course, and often defensive themselves, but some such conclusion seems called for because the torsions I've tried to describe are associated with 'modernity', and because, for the Conversation to have persisted so many millennia, 'subject' and 'object' must once have been neither so voracious nor so feeble, and so capable of some kind of fruitful, Conversation-enabling mutual existence.

Almost everywhere one looks there are signs that, whatever might be meant by 'lost unity' or 'the search for reality', it is felt as something quite definite, as an almost sensory absence of a nameless X from modern life. The very structure of the human world has risen into everyday consciousness as a problem quite recently, though literary formulations of it can be found as far back (at least) as the mid-nineteenth century. An anecdotal way of looking at this might be to begin with George Orwell's description of England as a nation of dedicated hobbyists (gardening, stamp-collecting, jam-making ...), with examples all the way from the industrious (Victorian statesmen also being giants in the fields of mycology or lepidoptery or expert sailors or members of the Alpine Club) to the vaguely eccentric (like Wemmick in *Great Expectations*). Has this altered at all? Have some modern hobbies not become, so to speak, sources of identity? Devoting one's time to the Aetherius Society (which believes Jesus to be alive and well on, I think, Saturn) or the Liberal Democrats might be extreme instances, but, even so, I think there is a case for saying that as *hobbies* change into *lifestyle choices* then perhaps they reflect a feeling that identity has to be supplemented, that perhaps the traditional structures do not offer quite as much solidity as they did. Perhaps also we are beginning to try to impose ourselves on ordinary life with such vigour as almost to force it to live up to our expectations. Did our grandparents feel the rage for fulfilment and authenticity that we do? The excitement of the modern world is such that it might mask any faint feeling of oddity at the sight of many of us trying to *garner* reality with the steady perseverance of a shrew wolfing insects. The Brad Pitt film *Fight Club* was said recently by its star to be "against numbness". I wonder if we're not more aware now of the possibility of numbness than we were.

If we asked for evidence of a desire for the 'sensation of reality' in today's world, where might we find it?

In travelling: the search for authenticity might lead one to tracking Sir Aurel Stein or simply to an undiscovered Ionian café where they still serve that marvellous lemon-scented liqueur which your friends have never heard of. In each case the sensations of return and discovery-for-oneself are exhilarating. In nostalgia: whether the new phenomenon of 'interactive' museums, like the Jorvik Centre, or software enabling us to 'walk' around ancient Karnak; both of which from this point of view, are pretty-much-desperate attempts to recover the *mattedness*, the *definiteness* of the past. In autobiography: whether 'literary' or encountered in creative-writing classes or reminiscence therapy, the implied aim is to break through the crust of accreted assumptions about ourselves to the reality, the kernel. 'Heritage' and family-trees are part of this. This has much in common with: Revisionism of all kinds (though chiefly historical) – think of the 'Reputations' series on television. Reinterpretation of historical events or episodes has become the fashion - Tyrannosaurus Rex as a scavenger, Shakespeare as a Catholic, Hitler's homosexuality ... there is a frothing-over of reinterpretations which demands consideration. Even things like the Atkins Diet follow this pattern. Leaving aside the undoubted human passion for truth (an ambiguous gift anyway), I think this froth reflects the idea that, whereas the past was layered and spotted with myth, the present is clean and for the first time can see the past clearly. What I am pointing to is a double notion: that (1) truth is more available now to us than before, and (2) that if the sensation of rooted, sensual truth is difficult to find amongst the signs and the maxims, the statements and perspectives and the siren calls, then relief can be provided by the exhilarating sense of breakthrough which revisionism affords. I am not denigrating works of revisionist history. I am suggesting that the hunger for them has a complex motive.

'Thick' history and anthropology: where constitutional and march-of -time history are 'thin' and summative, 'thick' history gorges on the local and ephemeral and specific: cognitive archaeology, Richard Hutton, Carlo Ginzburg, Montaillou, Myddle. Thick history is the determination to be adequate to the domestic particularity of events. And the growing desire for thickness in history reveals an impatience with normalised and so unreal accounts, an appetite for recovery. And also in shopping: products promising to reveal the 'real you', make the most of yourself, recapture the harmony, express your individuality. Many earlier 'fashion statements' in Norbert Elias' *The Civilising Process* seem to appeal to the desire to fit in, be appropriate; perhaps ours do, too, but they're couched more in terms of standing out and being faithful to the authenticity of 'who you are'; that is, exposing the shining *reality* that has been masked by habit or fear.

And in language itself. Candidates for the most characteristic set of words of our time might well include those centred on 'relation', 'relative' or 'relationship', their cumulative noise stressing with unnecessary vigour the quality and extent (or even existence) of the strands of connection that bind us, or do not bind us, to our world; but my own nap selection would be the bland-sounding but highly-charged set based on Latin *res*. Real, the real, reality, really, really?, realism, realistic, real ale, real estate, real time, real money, 'it's the real thing', for real, in reality, in the real world, magic realism, naïve realism, socialist realism, reality principle, surreal, hyperreal, virtual reality, realising one's assets or potential or situation or what must be done or the truth, realising vision in action, or where your best interests lie. Reality is invoked as a guarantee of faith: Are you for real? I felt real (really) bad about him/her/it. Really and truly? Get real! [A bar in Durham City, 'Reality-X', started me thinking about this: reality lies through that door, not on these windswept cobbles.] This family of words and phrases, which help carry us on and through the perplexities of modern times in a thousand or ten thousand ways, has burgeoned, according to the NSOED [19], since the early or mid eighteenth century - ie, since the first social changes wrought by industrialisation. They seem, perhaps, to testify to a floating and unmentionable doubt, a twice-shy caution, concerning the fidelity of words and even their possibility of reference: who is this with whom I talk? Are his words the same as mine? How can I trust this unfamiliar or suddenly-precipitated situation? One thing communication technology has certainly done is to *dramatise* or *foreground* doubts such as these. Doubt is, of course, proper to the Conversation, as is uncertainty. But perhaps we are reaching a point where completely radical doubting can impel us to correspondingly radical certainties. A doubtfulness so radical would be absolutely new in human affairs.

It is in the nature of such things that several, or all, of these sources of evidence for anxiety about 'the real' may be clearly fake, or defensive, and not a simple and spontaneous reaction against something we feel is denying us natural certainty and groundedness. Travel and shopping, for instance, are extremely vulnerable to accepting a manufactured sense of reality as a substitute; that is, wanting the sensation of 'reality' without confronting what it is that makes us want it [20]. But their cumulative impact, despite that, surely demands to be taken seriously.

The sense of unreality we are noting here, and the glossiness of flattened surfaces we noted earlier, are, therefore, not confined to the creepier recesses of education and psychology. They are, I think, proper to our thinking of ourselves as *modern*, the feeling that we have somehow broken through to a higher, airier place, a plateau. Some recent triumphs of science (eg the Human Genome project) contribute to this by egging us on to the idea that the replacement of all that might seem congested, maze-like, arcane or hidebound isn't far away. A random-ish list of such shaggy anomalies might include differences between generations, legal archaisms, town centres still riddled with burgage plots and winding streets, burdensome protocol, and public or even private ritual. (How scared we are of seeming, for instance, 'stilted' or 'affected', 'stuffy' or 'artificial'. I do not say that what we mean by these things was necessarily *good*, simple word, but that they necessarily hid, or allowed to be expressed in other ways, some kinds of liberty or ability that we may be blind to. Odd that an age so obsessed by style as the present seeks to obliterate a range of quite definite styles.) We've become accustomed to the gratifying sensation of having supplanted difficulty with ease, gradualness with speed, narrowness with breadth, texture with glissando. In the little part of this world to do with education, the lens that is education magnifies, again, some of this anxiety-born, anxiety-denying rapture: hopelessly obstructive snags to beatific plans of 'raising standards' cause a kind of infantile outrage, regressive apoplexy, in some quarters, simply because they tell against this superstition.

16. Fearing unreality in ourselves, we paper it over with images of perfection and harmony.

There is, as it happens, a good deal of support for the idea that glossiness and surface-awareness are useful ways in to the understanding of our century. It seems as if, as a society presses against some critical point of complexity, it simultaneously reacts against complexifying its self-awareness, and offers to its members instead a series of desperate – but also immensely powerful – visions of simplicity. But the value of such simplicity has changed quite recently. The clutter of sign and effect which we noticed earlier is no longer as it seemed in the 'fifties, a morally-comprehensible example of 'self-indulgent consumerism' (see, for example, F R Leavis and, in educational terms, David Holbrook). A gradually more psychological version of it has arisen, as of a kind of phantasmagorical thinness pervading not so much, perhaps, our private lives, which if we are lucky are still dense, matted, and responsive, but our life together as citizens. (That is not quite the same as the life of 'public debate'.) I am thinking, for instance, of the spectacle of modern life granted to the situationist philosopher Raoul Vaneigem – he spoke [21] of an

> "economy which cannot stop making us consume more and more, and to consume without respite is to change illusions at an accelerating pace which gradually dissolves the illusion of change. We find ourselves alone, unchanged, frozen ... behind the waterfall of gadgets, family cars, and paperbacks."

I want to pick out the word 'waterfall' here. For myself, I do not see a Wordsworthian fount of being, but something shimmering and hypnotic which *passes us by*, fails, supremely, to connect with our being. The prisoner of the waterfall is stayed, enthralled. Wittgenstein: "A *picture* holds us captive ... we are unable to turn our eyes away from it" [22]. "A culture which encourages mass consumption encourages narcissism, a disposition to see the world as a mirror" [23] – Christopher Lasch's image of the shimmering hypnosis is connected with what he calls an ideology of survivalism, whose leading tactic is and must be tunnel vision, a shortening of perspective, that is, which eliminates difference and otherness as too much of a risk. This tranced quality and these images of phantasmagoric thinness are the loss of the power to distinguish between illusion and reality, or, putting it another way, the image of the desire to collapse them.

The great symbol of this is perhaps the fantasy of what Jean Baudrillard [24] calls the 'celibate machine'. For Baudrillard, the computer is much more an attempt to bring into reality a fantasy of perfection than it is an attempt to make living

94

easier or business more profitable. He refuses the term 'artificial intelligence': "the computer is devoid of intelligence because it is devoid of artifice" – that is, in it there is no gap between illusion and reality; indeed, the very term 'reality' is alien to it, as alien as the sensation of being an angel or a bat is to us, because its being is to refuse to grant reality to anything outside its own operations. It is the 'celibate' machine precisely because of this – it "can never succumb to its object", and, more shortly, "it has no other". To that extent it is like an autistic mind which has closed off the possibility of exchange in order to function. The important point here is not that Artificial Intelligence cannot exist but that our fascination with its possibility is a telling consequence of that feeling of spellbound impotence in the face of the waterfall and the vision of shimmering and imprisoning crystal thinness it connotes. It is, whether it can be said to exist or not, a fantasy: a vision or version of ourselves which we have produced in unconscious reaction to what we think of ourselves. Forget, for the moment, its benefits, or its interestingness [25] – they merely help to explain the way some people think it treasonous to speak of A I as a fantasy. To consider it as a phenomenon in our mental life, our ways of being together, is to say: we have invested so much of our confidence and energy in the image of the celibate machine because it gives us something *psychic*, rather than material, and that is the illusory faith in a perfect and impassive functioning, almost a magical functioning, in the face of the torrent of unintelligibility which we have created. The computer has no other because there is no gap between reality and its operations, and therefore no reality: it exactly, completely and perfectly performs what it must and what else there is does not exist for it. It is perhaps the most compelling image of collapse, of the effacement of the living gap of uncertainty, that we have, and in so being it is an image of the annulment of the Conversation [26].

Some of this phantasmagoria can be traced back to Marx. Whatever the roots of his attempt to erect an uncertainty-proof and self-collapsed version of history into a system, he was certainly a sensitive register of the impact on humanity of the modern world: *"If man is to be man, and his relationship to the world a human one ..."* – had it ever been thought necessary to pose the question before? [27] 'Phantasmagoria' is actually his word for the puzzled relations of illusion and reality I have been trying to describe. He makes the same point in other, perhaps less appealing words: production not only creates "an object for the subject, but a subject for the object". In making our living through the ages, that is, we reach a point where what we have made of the world is so overwhelmingly complex and so insistent in its calls on us that we reshape our minds to accommodate ourselves to it [28]. The result is entrancement.

And that, clearly, is a major bit of defensiveness. Not wanting to understand this ('bad faith') hasn't been expressed better than by Fredric Jameson (29): "Alienation experienced as exhilaration". Looking out from our plateau, those airy uplands we are told we inhabit, we see a glittering landscape, the fairyland of modernity, which we don't wish to acknowledge we've substituted for something almost impossible to characterise. Despite this, in one sense it faithfully reflects a nagging sense of something being not quite right, because we feel obscurely that a great deal depends on keeping up appearances, on willing the fairyland in existence.

17. The magical sense of ourselves is a way of reconciling us to the fairy land of signs and maxims.

Indeed it does. Where would Britain go from here without the exhilarating buoyancy and sense of purpose, openness, responsibility and political correctness that has so suddenly welled up from the mud of Thatcherism? And to put the point in Education terms: no political change conceivable at the moment will be able to stop 'willing the fairyland' (mainly because social changes wrought by technology are only in their infancy). No government will be able to stop talking about raising standards, nor will they be able to stop doing so in divorced subjective/objective, emotion/rigour terms. (Understand, I *am* not criticising the desire to give our children as good an education as possible; indeed I think it's even more urgent now, because of the disastrous way in which we *talk* about it. I *am* criticising the usually unacknowledged purposes and mental habits hidden in 'Raising Standards' and encouraged by it.) Governments will not be able to do this because they, like 'Education', follow change rather than initiate it in other than a trivial sense, and in following it they must incorporate /deform/assuage (and even express) emotional resistances to change. The trick, for Governments, will continue to be keeping belief in it going while not really wanting it to happen (because then it would be over, and because it will always be impossible to remodel the teaching force in ways that could make it happen *as it is supposed to*) and while also simultaneously praising teachers for those automatic yearly rises in SATS, GCSE and 'A'-level passes, and university firsts, and reprimanding them in all manner of politically convenient ways.

Tricks such as this use 'magic', and in several senses 'magic' has been the theme of this section. Unconscious emotional defences could be said to be a very primitive form of magical transformation (and, even, unconscious recognition of these defences one source of the universal fascination with magic). Magical language seeps into the means by which we articulate our situation, and magical or fantasy images (the celibate machine, the maturity of the millennium, the gadarene onrush of communicativeness, the shimmering horopter ...) deconstruct or remodel the relations of 'subject' and 'object'. And the brittle glossiness of magical effect illuminates the 'signs and maxims' we have taken for the Conversation.

Spaces

18. At times of uncertainty, we are especially vulnerable to images of magical certainty, and intolerant of uncertainty.

I was on a walking holiday in the Wolds with my brother when I began to think about this bit. It was a bright, crisp morning in November, and the thickly-grassed chalk was riven by narrow tawny dales, gleaming fallow in the light. When we sat down beside a long deep hedge to smoke and fight for the map, the intensest colour for miles around was his preposterous purple hat, with ear-flaps like Budgie the Helicopter, until a roving shaft of sunlight pounced on the hedge and lit up thousand on thousand of deep red berries, all fat and full and brilliant. Jed, possibly wanting to divert attention from this hat of his, said, *"Look at that – they all sparked up together. You'd think the whole lot were -* **unanimous***"*.

That word, perceptive and accurate as it is, still seems to me curious. Why should we think in terms of *mind* about something so relatively low on the intellectual ladder as a hedge? It's as if we are ready to attend to and compare ourselves to anything which offers a picture of a way of being distinct from and alien to our own. Olaf Stapledon (science fiction writer and popular philosopher) has a similar moment in his 1937 novel *Star Maker*. He's set himself possibly the most unpromising novelistic task in the history of writing, that of describing believably the evolution of species after species of quasi-human, on galaxy after galaxy; the 'human spirit' materialises in many unconventional forms, once as a blue fish, I seem to remember, and certainly once as some kind of vegetable. This form proves attractive to the human spirit, which finds it difficult to move on after becoming acquainted with what Stapledon calls "the ecstasy of the vegetal experience".

Unanimity, ecstasy ... is there a kind of mindless relief from being human and individual that we can sometimes imagine? Can freedom from uncertainty and encompassment be sometimes felt as a burden, as well as a gift? If the ability to picture a kind of being without differentiation, or even a time before differentiation, is something which we all have, then it is akin to that collapsing of difference we saw as an imaginative defence against threat, and so to a whole array of attitudes such as nostalgia. I don't mean, of course, that my brother was succumbing to something like that when he suddenly saw the red berries as if they were a million-centred unconscious oneness; rather that what his imagination seized on was a kind of momentary vision which, like all human thought, can serve many purposes. In normal conditions it is just, as it were, the respect paid by highly-conscious humanity to another form of life. Something that might get us thinking about humanity, that is.

Such a vision of life-without-differentiation may be something we measure ourselves against. I am thinking here of the fact that undifferentiation, or a dead harmony, has been repeatedly pictured as something which achievement, individuality, defines itself by escaping from, and consequently as an imaginative source of nostalgia. The Dutch psychiatrist J H van den Berg [30] interpreted the Mona Lisa as the picture of the new Renaissance 'inner self', arising ambiguously (hence the smile) from the all-embracing totality of late medieval Europe. Christianity itself has been understood (by Nicolas Berdyaev) [31] as tearing through the exhausted trammels of myth into history, revealing the 'freedom of good' and liberating humanity from a 'spellbound harmony with nature'.

Because what we have discarded in becoming ourselves is pictured as a 'spellbound harmony', it is also the way we can tend to picture escape from individuality and variousness. The Frankfurt philosopher Theodor Adorno recognises this:

> "The picture of a happy identity between subject and object is today no more than a lie … The undifferentiated state before subjectivity's formation was the dread of the blind web of nature, of myth; it was in protest against it that the great religions had their truth-content." [32]

I'm drawing attention to these rather daunting considerations because undifferentiation has the *same pattern* as some of the observations made earlier. Images of magical harmony lurk in all our minds, and not very far down, either. And some uses to which these images of escape from duality (for that is what we're talking about) are put can be remarkably violent. The novelist Ernst von Salomon was a powerful and rather sinister talent who, in *Die Fragebogen* (1951) – answers to 131 questions posed by the Allied Military Government in their denazification programme – turns the questionnaire into a farce by the 'cynical and contemptuous frankness' [33] with which he writes of his past. Von Salomon, despite his name, was in his youth a savage and exultant participant in the *Freikorps*, fighting against the Berlin Spartacists, the Russians, Esthonians, and Poles, in the years immediately following the Great War. The *Freikorps*, volunteer political mercenaries and ex-soldiers of the far right, were possessed by fury at the signing of the Armistice (the 'stab in the back' of the German Army) and at the growing confidence of the Left (Jewish, Communist, and decadent, in their eyes). In 1930 von Salomon, aged only 28, published his first novel, *Die Geächteten* ('The Outlaws') and displayed there with extraordinarily bitter clarity the nihilistic *esprit de corps* with which he and his 'brothers' waged their ecstatic revenge:

> "This stale, abominable world was to be annihilated ... There were no people any more, only masks ... Explosives should be put under this decayed, stinking pap, so that the muck spatters on the moon ... The earth should be clean shaven ... Perhaps a new race will come from the moon, or Mars; the earth should have a meaning once again."

That piece of frighteningly intense blackness is about the most extreme example of a detestation of encounter [34] that I am aware of. It is not so much the enjoyment of brutality – which needs an existing enemy – that this extract shows, but an almost ascetic desire for cleanliness [35], in a sense for there never to have been an enemy. Its sensuous intensity, its visionary energy, refuse encounter on any ground but its own: in the autism or solipsism of its rage it is undiscussable. To put the point in a different way (ie to try to meet it on different ground), can you imagine buying him a drink and saying, "Now, Ernst, if you just listen a moment, there's another point of view I'd like to –". I wasn't sure what a boggled imagination felt like until beginning that sentence, but I am now.

Where Ernst von Salomon connects with normal people is in that momentary glimpse of another world, reality shorn of actuality: fantasising 'dead harmony', imagining the earth clean-shaven, giving credence to rogue subjectivity, have a close family resemblance to more familiar, less demented collapsings of difference, as well as to the simple and fruitful 'respect paid to another form of life' like the unanimity and the vegetable ecstasy. That resemblance isn't lessened by saying there are no grades in dementia, or no step-by-step progression from the frustration we can all feel at times to the Salomonic heights.

I don't know if we could call such an annulment of otherness a distinctly modern disease; perhaps the awareness of it is modern, as we have grown more sensitive to the ambiguity of visions. Adorno's diagnosis, in the 1950s, was that the modern world was increasingly subject to that kind of magical fantasy because it had, in effect, overvalued subjectivity [36]; that there was a "bias to the subject" which emerged in every facet of life from political theory to leisure pursuits. The only alternative to this privileging of the subject, to the encroachment of the subjective on the object, would be some version of equality or mutuality. (A privileging of the object could not, presumably, mean anything at all.) Adorno's word for this interexistence, the fruitful equipoise of subject and object, is 'constellation': a shaping, that is, of the relations between the two (and what he calls the 'collective subject') which includes their distancing. It is a spatial metaphor for an unprivileged mutuality.

Could the same not be said, more concretely perhaps, of human relations as they can be when not undergoing all the varieties of nervous distortion to which they are notoriously prone? Separateness, but mutual influence; distance, but regard and reflection and interest; togetherness, in arrangement, but individuality, in personal existence. Does this need saying? Is it not almost so recognisable a truth that we have no need of it? Rather, I feel, we have need particularly of recognisable truths; and the more so because recognising truth in words does not mean we are not capable of garbling it in action. That is a consequence of the liberty of conscience which I am trying to make space for in our crowded arena of certainties. Liberty of conscience means among other things that the uncertainty which we live in and which is our life is also, at times, expressed in contradiction, or what to a monocular vision might appear contradiction. The distance established in a constellation of subject and object is the spaciousness that allows for reality, but also the non-identity which makes inconsistency possible. That gap is the condition of sanity, and it underlies what I have called 'uncertainty' or 'letting-be'.

19. There are examples of a reaction against this: they indicate the fruitfulness of uncertainty.

My attempt hasn't been to chronicle whatever has happened to the letting-be, or capacity to live in, without deforming, the uncertainty and inexhaustibility of the Conversation. Rather it has been to indicate something of why and in what ways it can be deformed, and to hazard that at some level even our continued deforming expresses an awareness of what is being so deformed. I think that, among or beyond the instances I have given of that kind of spiritual tinkering, there is, even in the same places, some growing awareness that an abeyance, a kind of abstention from the possessiveness of the subjective and the fantastic, is called for. Adorno's privileging of the subjective is here recognised and combated. The response the language makes – that insisting on the recuperative balm of 'reality' I mentioned – is one glimpse of this. Others are scattered in many places, sometimes not instantly recognisable for what they are. As the world closes in and reduces its variousness, for instance, and habitats, languages [37] and ancient forms of life disappear , there is evidence that we are literally, not metaphorically, being diminished by that – "we need the tonic of wildness" in Thoreau's words [38]. 'Wildness' perhaps corresponds here to the not-ourselves, the rich, resistant and untraversable object which Adorno saw as parasitised by the subject. In this connection, the biologist E O Wilson and the sociologist Roger Caillois [39] independently speculate that the very existence of incomparable modes of life (the tree, the insect) formed, by reflection, our archaic sense of humanity. We came to a partial understanding of ourselves by pondering our difference from them. But that harmonised mode of life can still make us nostalgic for it. The unanimity of the berries on the Wolds and the ecstasy of vegetal existence testify to the continuing natural attraction of such images [40].

In a seemingly very different field, language itself and poetry have come to be understood as, in a sense, *made of* and *making* spatiality and difference; and not, that is, 'made of' expressivity or subject-matter [41]. Although this is too vast a topic to plummet into here, and although it is of course rash to express it so simply, that width, distinction and heterogeneity which is here appealed to is (I would say) the *very same* diversity which Thoreau and Wilson articulate: the contrary, that is, of the smothering subjective. Even objects as such have been linked to this developing awareness. For Hannah Arendt [42] "the things of the world have the function of stabilising human life", and through them human beings can "retrieve ... their identity". "Bless you, things", writes Iris Murdoch in *The Nice and the Good*, daringly for a conspicuously weighty stylist, but perhaps registering the shock of seeing again the huge fateful simplicity of the object. "To restore silence is the role of objects" (Samuel Beckett, in *Molloy*). I'd interpret that silence as the peace of mutuality and difference; recall the clamour, urgency and shallowness of those calls upon us which can wreathe our speaking in such paralysing filaments.

Difference, and yet simplicity; recognition, and yet uncertainty; these are constants of the spacious images of abeyance which seem to answer to our need and to be emblematic of the Conversation. The therapist R D Laing once said, in a television interview, a very simple-sounding thing – that "the therapist ... lets be" [43]. The spaciousness of this is twofold. Firstly, it is not limited in meaning merely to (for instance), 'leaves well alone', but extends to 'allows to be', or if that sounds too patrician, 'refuses to deform'. And, secondly, it acknowledges spaciousness, or variety, itself, preserves it as part of the reconstitution of right relations, and instinctively refuses to claim possession of otherness, of another's space. We can feel almost tangibly the sensuous tact of such a refusal – such an abeyance – in Keats' marvellous (and spatially-conscious) description of negative capability [44]: that is, "when a man is capable of being in uncertainties, mysteries, and doubts, without any irritable reaching after fact and reason". I don't want to be misunderstood here: Keats is hardly denying the value of fact and reason, but he is denying that any old use of fact and reason, any old unexamined desperation for their comfort and security, is necessarily responsible or wise, and he is denying that they represent by themselves, as it were, what we are *for*. They do not substitute in times of need for the Conversation.

20. Uncertainty is a thrilling contact with the unknowable:

I want now to try to indicate what this abeyance or uncertainty may feel like – literally, to make *sense* of it; which is perhaps at least as important as attempting to define it (thankless task). The closest I can get is a sense of balanced equipoise, that distancing and equal weighting of the known and unknown which the constellation suggested. I shall try to convey this sense by discussing, firstly, the endings of two great novels, and, secondly, a word invented for a very germane purpose by a very easily misunderstood writer, Samuel Taylor Coleridge.

In the 1868 edition of *Great Expectations*, Dickens ends with a beautiful neutral-tinted sobriety:

> "*I took her hand in mine, and we went out of the ruined place; and, as the morning mists had risen long ago when I first left the forge, the evening mists were rising now, and in all the broad expanse of tranquil light they showed to me, I saw no shadow of another parting from her*". (Ch 59)

The 1861 version ("I saw the shadow of no parting from her") was, very slightly, more certainly a 'happy ending', but both are a radical change from the ending as originally written. There, Pip and Estella meet only briefly and accidentally, and the final sentence reads:

> "*I was very glad afterwards to have had the interview; for, in her face and in her voice, and in her touch, she gave me the assurance that suffering had … given her a heart to understand what my heart used to be.*"

Why the change? Partly, perhaps, to avoid the suspicion of *Schadenfreude*, vengefulness, in Pip's voice ('Now she knows what it's like'). More than that, though, a novel so ruefully aware of the possibilities of mistaken judgment and of the necessity of reparation and hope would be horribly dented by the hammering home of a Moral such as, in the words of one critic, 'sombre recognition of the irreparability of human action' (That'll teach him!).

But Dickens trod a very fine line here. He gets rid of moralistic finality, yes; but he also refuses to leave us with a complementary certainty, that of Pip and Estella happy ever after. Gratitude and acceptance, no more. They leave the 'ruined place', like Adam and Eve, for the uncertainty of more life, and we leave them in an almost breathless, tranced moment in which, without it being stated, the full responsibility of further, various, uncertain life can be felt. Their humanised vigilance would be switched-off, curtailed, by either of the other two alternatives, happiness ever after or lifelong separation.

Hans Castorp's ending in Thomas Mann's *The Magic Mountain* is similarly rich and indeterminate. He has been becalmed in an Alpine sanatorium for seven years, rather like one of those enchanted mortals, Thomas the Rhymer perhaps, who get caught up in fairyland. Now he descends to the plains to take his part in the Great War:

> *"Was he hit? He thought so, for a moment. A great clod of earth struck him on the shin; it hurt, but he smiles at it. Up he gets and staggers on, limping on his earth-bound feet, all unconsciously singing ... and thus, in the tumult, in the rain, in the dusk, vanishes from our sight.*

> *Farewell, honest Hans Castorp! Your tale is told ... after all, it was your story, it befell you, you must have more in you than we thought ... Farewell, whether you live or die!"*

The switching of tenses, the odd, self-conscious elegy, the flourished uncertainty of judgment, together announce - what? the ultimate futility of his escape into self-discovery? No. The heroism of his spirit, stumbling into that 'universal feast of death'? Not likely, not with that clod of earth and that undemonstrative word 'tumult'. We're left with a lesson – not a moral, but an enacted, pictured lesson – in partial understanding and its being woven gradually into the dense texture of life until it vanishes; the reach of understanding into that indescribable tumultuous dusk is not very far, and *yet we have no sense of loss,* rather of an enlivening contact. Like the Dickens, there's a kind of excited absence here, and I'd like to link that to the fact that both of them refuse to lapse into a vision, into some smothering clarity which obliterates otherness and difference and absence. This isn't a vision but a vignette and it is a really wonderful thing that vignettes should be so much more live, tonic, possible, various and real than visions are.

That avoidance of finality, in these cases over-apt moralism (Dickens) and smothering 'vision' (Mann), seem to me to be akin to tact,[45] respect, refusal to deflect or deform. Their tonic effect is that they allow us to feel, amongst other things, a liberating and un-self-centred interest in the world we cannot hope to encompass. Neither is overdetermined: that is the great blessing of uncertainty.

21. Uncertainty creates spaces in understanding where solutions deny them.

These instances 'make sense of' uncertainty, *literally*, by showing us what it feels like. Another way might be to create spaces between the word 'uncertainty' and other words. We owe the idea of the fruitfulness of *desynonymy*, of untangling lazily-equated words, to the maligned Coleridge. He has been accused many times, starting with Carlyle, of being afraid of difference and uncertainty; of being, that is, a neurotic systematiser with a mania for definition, for identifying, for tightening down each element of life and thought into an impregnable arrangement of abstractions. Where Dr Johnson, I think, could be considered an arch-systematiser by training and by temperament who nevertheless became himself, the most tonic and dramatic of all writers who aren't Shakespeare, by *resisting* his own need for system, Coleridge would have loved to be such a great collapser, a man of no uncertainty whatsoever, but couldn't manage it. His never-failing interest in the world forbade it. And so he continually throws off ideas which work against collapsing and identity, one of which is desynonymy. Desynonymy, from our point of view, creates spaces between words, and so frees responsive thought. Coleridge's most well-known bit of desynonymising is, of course, the space between 'fancy' and 'imagination', but there are many others. One relevant to our purpose here is that between 'unity' (collapsed identity, eg of the fantasy of undifferentiated subject and object) and 'union', which is similar to what I have here called 'mutuality'. There are desynonymies begging to be made in teaching, too: 'knowledge' and 'awareness', for instance; and 'accountability' and 'responsibility' are often equated instantly in educational thinking, yet a moment's thought will reveal profound and important differences between them. Perhaps 'a child's potential' could be segregated from 'could do better'[46]. I'd like to distinguish 'uncertainty' from one or two ambiguous neighbours, also. By 'uncertainty' I do not mean, for instance, simply being tolerant. Toleration might look like the contrary of intolerance, but they both reserve the sense that we have the right to withhold or impose action or judgment as we see fit. To tolerate something might also be to neutralise it, as we saw when kebabbing and marginalising were under discussion. Similarly, by valuing uncertainty I do not mean merely abstaining from the effort to understand, or being indifferent (uncertainty is receptive, where indifference isn't). Uncertainty of the type I have in mind means, at the least, enjoying the sensation of inexhaustibility in what and whom we encounter, and, more than that, recognising that genuineness *lives nowhere else* but in that sensation. If we can exhaust it, it's not really there. This must mean allowing ourselves to be inexhaustible, untraversable, to others: we are, each of us, much less easily-traversed than we dare to believe is admissible, even though, deep down unless we are truly damaged, each of us is aware of our own richness, our hidden trove. As soon, then, as we begin to think 'uncertainty' we think it in terms of mutuality, variousness, and being unsurrounded. Unlike the celibate machine, uncertainty is *faithful to its other*, strange though that may sound to modern ears. This is what

I take R D Laing to mean – uncertainty is the only way of allowing the 'other' to become itself.

Another pairing of words I find too close for comfort is 'answer' and 'solution'. An answer is partial, a response, a recognition, almost an offering, but a solution, I am afraid, is a perfectionist fantasy. To solve the truth of a person, a school, even a lesson, just as much as to solve the 'riddle of the universe', is essentially *giving up* on the possibility of responding to that person, school, lesson or universe. Anything genuine is an answer; I'd hope this piece of writing is an answer to some questions posed of teachers. But it is very far from a *solution* [47]. It's offered only as one way of acknowledging[48] ourselves among others, and is much too blankly simple, and figurative, to be anything other than a picture. This must be so because, in thinking about the Conversation, we see with increasing confidence that we are actually far richer and more complex, less cleanly-edged and more indefinite in our boundaries (like those of the Yemen) than we are often brave enough to acknowledge. It takes a kind of courage to acknowledge the freedom of others from your interpreting in a way that preserves their freedom. So no one interpretation can be anything more than partial, provisional, exemplary, figurative. There can be no *solutions* because there can strictly be no traverse of our rich uncertainty, no vantage-point from which to survey and triangulate it. In place of solutions there is *answering*, human, provisional, and needing answer itself, and, in place of certainty, fruitfulness or its lack.

Questions in education, then, are vexed because we are vexed, at there being no end, no solution, at the impossibility of judgment and the impertinence of its pretence. Our vexation at the urgency with which it calls to us tempts us to connive at the pretence of its finality and so gift ourselves the illusion of strength. We are vexed because we have allowed ourselves to be both over-optimistic and over-pessimistic, the first because thinking in terms of *problems* allows us to fantasise *solutions*, and the second because the end result is always a disabling disillusion. (For these, read: the uninspirational faith in inspiration of such institutional visions as that of Ofsted, and the caricatures of staffroom folklore, the hopelessness of the clinically-judged teacher. Perhaps the circle is completed by the second feeding back into the first.)

How dare I assert there are no solutions? Surely I must be 'simply' another bloody-minded teacher fighting an antediluvian battle against change? That is the effect of disillusion. It makes us caricature others, and, turning back on ourselves, we too are caricatured by our effort to evade disillusion. By contrast, I am confident that there *is* hope in education, and always has been, because education is part of the integrity of the Conversation, part of what the Conversation *means*. (It would be futile to try to imagine the Conversation *without* something corresponding to 'education'...). And by the same token, 'hope' is not the antonym of 'disillusion'; 'illusion' is that antonym. We must deantonymise hope and disillusion (if I can be allowed that word) because, in my usage here, hope belongs to the Conversation – it is part of the way we have always been alive, that is – and is not a contemptuous name for a kind of unrealistic and vain wishing. That vanity is illusion, its antonym disillusion, and (like 'problem' and 'solution') they are both the creatures of premature certainty. They are great wooden caricatures, like Punch and Judy, not conductive realities. That certainty which animates them pretends to traverse the unknowable, to rectify the borders of Yemen; it issues in brief, perhaps impressive and seductive, attempts to tame the wilderness (Thoreau's 'wildness'), to lasso the uncontrollable. Xerxes the Great, preparing his invasion of Greece, is said to have vowed to make the boundaries of Persia coincide with the sky: a belief in magic and an intolerance of uncertainty lead us to such pronouncements of conceited drivel, in education as elsewhere.

Solutions reek of caution, a fear of everything they cannot lasso, just as much as of a kind of quixotic rashness. Solutions seem to be the only *point* of there being problems. Like the essays of a student I once taught, they carefully exclude everything that seems – at first blush – as if it ought to be irrelevant, and proceed only by that method. This girl, faced with Tourneur's *The Revenger's Tragedy*, wanted a key to open it – ideally, a probing interview with Tourneur, but, failing that, some rules of transformation that would enable solutions to come: this, that and that show Tourneur's intentions, that, this and this are ways he succeeded, or failed. Then one could stop thinking or responding or engaging or being puzzled. Keys or techniques of the kind she imagined to exist could in principle be used in exactly the same manner by any native English speaker who was present and conscious in lesson time. But they obtrude between student and teacher, and between student and text, so that roles are predetermined and spaces are squeezed. In a similar way, formulae, judgments, diagrams, magic spells, codes,[49] devices, indicators, profiles, place themselves *between* actor and action, subject and object, knower and known, person and person. They deform space, like gravity does, and they easily substitute for the natural exchange of genuineness, of answering, that ought to exist. In the case of the key-desiring student, they deformed her own relation to her learning: she found it difficult to understand why she wasn't doing brilliantly, and she found it almost impossible to think of literature as anything other than a set of puzzles whose solution is entirely external to oneself. Somewhere, it seems, a *respect for uncertainty* has leached away in these refusals of encounter. And if we are looking for tasks for education, then there surely is a great one: to break through the smooth wash of 'learning' of this key/problem/device/solution-obsessed kind.

22. Respecting uncertainty means distinguishing subjectivity from self-indulgence.

There has been a good deal about places, real or imagined, in these pages – the Wolds, the Yemeni Republic, the frame where Drama happens, the 'little world of education'; some of them are bad places - the fairyland of modernity, the suburbs of dissent, School X's theatre, the gulag. I have only just noticed this, and am wondering why it is. Could it be that those places or place-images which offer a sensation of spaciousness, the hospitality and difference of particular spaces, speak out against the suffocating atmosphere of collapse, completeness, traversable bounds? Difference and untraversed regions require, and are built of, space - abeyance, the reach of mutuality, letting-be are expressions of its peace. But collapsing difference requires the abolition of such spaciousness. Ernst von Salomon's clean-shaven earth (how glad I am that he can never read this) isn't really a space at all, but a unit or a point - spatiality was swept off it and blown at the moon. I suspect also that the tight exclusiveness of his *Freikorps* brotherhood, the Outlaws,[50] is a version of that hatred of difference and of the risks of uncertainty. School X's teaching force, clad in their uniforms and intoning their mantras of 'Good morning' rather than 'Hi' and 'clients' rather than 'parents' are a reflex of the same thing. On a different plane, certainly, but still - not trivial.

Those inexhaustible spaces which I am proposing as the true locus of the Conversation allow for something no less central to its spirit: the liberty of conscience alluded to above. One of the most misused manoeuvres in 'debate' is: You do not practise what you preach, so you have no right to preach. Stated clearly, this relies on the following assumption: One only has the right to preach what one is actually able to practise sincerely and consistently. By contrast, liberty of conscience, which some might regard as a hypocrites' charter, means that at the same time as creating the possibility of hypocrisy we also create the possibility of recognising truths which we can't embody, or live up to, or die for, or even bear in mind consistently. That strikes me as something to celebrate. More than that, we wouldn't be human without it. If hypocrisy is undesirable, then so is a heroic, narrow and stupid consistency, which, like its cousin Ofsted 'neurotic completeness', is founded on fear of encounter. Consistency as a general aim, rather than a fetish, is surely good: I'd be pretty hugely worried if I thought a really consistent inconsistency ran right through this essay. But to strip out 'consistency' and 'exactness' from the texture of living and paint them up as Punch and Judy - use them to fight one's insecure battles, I mean - is surely bad. Liberty of conscience is uncertain, certainly, but it isn't insecure. Liberty of conscience means that our possibility (in the Kierkegaardian sense used elsewhere in this book) and our necessity are not very or consistently congruent. The freedom of the Conversation flows from that. Such freedom allows us to let inexhaustibility and reality, for instance of another person, populate the spread of our personality, and allows us to reach into reality ourselves; at the same time our timid feelings of susceptibility to simple and total judgment are cancelled. But because we are thereby free, unknowable, in balance with what is not ourselves, we are *also* various, capable of development or regression, in a sense made of layers or levels of intensity of self which fade or brighten according to circumstances, the flow of the Conversation around and through us, and to our current placing within it. We are thus quite naturally able to differ from others *and ourselves* without prejudice to our integrity. This is what the charter of the hypocrites amounts to: we cannot always *know* what another's integrity or placing is like; the spacious differentiation that allows us to live means we have to live with the difference of others, and therefore their resistance to our 'knowledge'. They may fool us; we may fool ourselves, but, as I remarked above, we have a right to be wrong as well as a duty to be uncertain and that is something we must accept. It is a consequence of how we live in the Conversation. The heroically stupid consistency which is all that institutionalised judgment can register is, by contrast, homogeneous, a block, sharp-edged and revealing the same composition at each cut or view. It homogenises space. But it isn't a homogeneity we in fact possess; it isn't related to how we in fact acknowledge, explore, or love the world or each other. It isn't, therefore, what animates our education of each other, but is only the self-generated fantasy of something which seeks to overcome encounter, something worried by it and insecure in the face of it. That something comes perhaps from the bewilderment, anxiety and fears of unreality of the last century or so, and it is always attempting to pass itself off as objectivity. But *real* objectivity, as this section has tried to indicate, is only available to us in the terms of the Conversation. Objectivity itself, that condition which we saw the 'celibate machine' incapable of succumbing to, may in fact be presented to us chiefly through the form of *other people* – that is, within the Conversation.

That is clearly not the reputation which objectivity has. In the Babel of screaming, intoning and disconsolate muttering which can occasionally, in one's less good-humoured moments, seem favoured kinds of public utterance (and which, if you think about it, provide a thumbnail sketch of three cardinal ways to indulge in monologue), so-called 'objectivity' is set against so-called 'subjectivity' in an idle contest for supremacy. Their voices achieve ever greater apparent definition: "vivid and exciting self-expression" versus the inhibited and anally-retentive clods of the objective, or "self-indulgent babble" versus "grownup and practical" realism. How could any of this make even minimal sense? In a way, perhaps, we can be grateful to (say) Shirley Maclaine and Chris Woodhead for symbolising the issues in such an obligingly asinine form. We know by virtue of our humanity that life does not offer itself to us in anything like those terms. The combatants in this war of futility could not have pinned their colours to those masts if 'subject' and 'object' hadn't been severed from each other, and manipulated (Punch and Judy again) as if they were enemies. Once that had happened, all manner of conversational powerlessness and frustration could happen; the day of the instant put-down (and the instant caricature, the instant badmouthing, and the instant judgment and the instant fake victory) had arrived. A close friend told me a story recently of a fellow from his undergraduate years whose sole purpose in discussion was to wait (days, sometimes) until his opponent, for that's what he had to be, made some statement that could be said to be a contradiction of some other statement – when that happened, he had 'contradicted himself' and, by some mysteriously-operating retrospective process, made unworthy of consideration anything else he had said on the topic. In words I owe to my brother, this annoying person had 'nothing at stake' in the exchange. Similarly, cries of 'That's purely subjective!' (weak-kneed, sentimental, foolish, short-sighted …) and 'Nothing's going to change my mind, you fascist!' (hard, 'judgmental', no fun any more …) are blanket defences, fire-blankets if you like, sharing – and this is the point – the fear of the inexhaustibility of the Other. Here, both combatants are one. The knee-jerk realist fears the loneliness of selfhood, its mystery perhaps; the knee-jerk self-expressionist alike fears the encroachment of selves upon his guarded, landlocked, ready-for-action territory. (Or they are acting as if they do. Belief in such defences can hardly go very deep.) So how far apart *really* are the subjective and objective, as publicly proclaimed modes of being? Nobody could be both more self-indulgent and more fascist than Ernst von Salomon.

23. Not using 'subjective' and 'objective' responsibly allows the rogue subjective to run riot.

These usages, then, are highly suspect. When I have been speaking of subjectivity and objectivity, I have not been speaking of alternative beliefs or ways of presenting oneself so much as of notional components of life as we naturally live it. They must be distinct, but cannot be separate. They are not opposed, but neither must they be identified. To speak in such a way means that I must be deantonymising them, as well as desynonymising 'objectivity' as used here and as used by the instant realist.

It's here that the notorious book *Faking It* [51] falls down. Discussing education, it equates subjectivity and sentimentality, and prescribes a dose of objectivity. But the kind of objectivity it proposes, as I have tried to show, is only a rogue subjectivity masquerading as its opposite, which is easy to do once 'subject' and 'object' are denatured and taken as opposites. Chris Woodhead, reviewing the book favourably in the *Sunday Times* [52], writes:

> *"We have come to believe that our only duty is to our feelings. The world we inhabit has, as a consequence, ceased to be something mysteriously and stubbornly other. We have twisted it into shapes that appeal to our egotistic and sentimental longings, projected our comforting fantasies onto it."*

The slipperiness of 'debate' in this area is pretty conspicuous when one sees the closeness of Woodhead's terms to those used here. Something has, he says, made 'the world' less 'other' and allowed us to 'project fantasies' onto it. For Woodhead, this is subjectivity ('our feelings'). For me, it is *only those of our 'feelings' which have constructed a fake objectivity*. It is these feelings, distorted by pressure and anxiety, which 'project fantasy' and so have secretly migrated to what they project as the opposing camp, that of 'objectivity'. In the picture here presented, the real subjective remains where it was, as does the real objective; masking them are Woodhead's 'objective' (wishes and anxieties hiding from sight behind their factitious screen) and his 'subjective', a kind of ghostly scapegoat created from the unreal polarity of his version of the world. As I have written of them, the subject and the object are not, however, polarities but necessary partners which participate in one another, partake of each other in animating Oakeshott's Conversation.

On this reading, then, Woodhead's position is quite as 'subjective', in his *own* terms, as any of the most New Age unconformities he would so abhor (Ian Paisley confronted by a Tracey Emin exhibit ...). And that subjectivity of his is deeper than the glib 'subjectivity' he castigates. Not simply because it pretends it isn't, but because of the way it misshapes the whole sensation of mental space this section has (intermittently) focused upon. The space, and the flow across it of the Conversation, have been interrupted. The giant warring polarities (Gog and Magog, Punch and Judy) which have supplanted mutuality and equipoise allow no exchange of trust and of being because they are *not really different* – both are 'subjective'in Woodhead's use of the word. Consequently, Woodheadism doesn't give us what it promises, a stable framework by which we can know what we are doing, but precisely and surreptitiously damages any such framework. Everything in education is warped because of that.

That spaciousness and uncertainty which I have tried to picture ought to go some way, even now, to repairing these frameworks of understanding. Such a picture exposes the secret neurosis of all those words, those boo- and rah-words, which we flourish so readily and with so little real belief: stress, challenge, accountability, innovative, radical, descriptor, indicator, profile, achievement, performance, standard. It's not that none of them has meaning, but that *unless* they are ballasted, stretched, counterpoised by words still wet with life they *can have* no meaning, so they can't be experienced, or felt, or lived. And that means that the only way they can be propped up is by *not meaning them*, another curious but expressive result of misshaping and distorting the spaces of understanding. They are invested with a magical stasis which allows them to be leached of meaning. (It also makes them difficult to write of without also discussing the whole topic of how we understand each other in these superstitious times.)

It is the spurious clarity of these words which offers parents of the children we teach that misleading sense of being involved in a national enterprise. Exposing it will clearly, then, be massively resisted, but the apparent objectivity masking their real subjectivity, and the messages they preach - that truths, lessons, schools, teachers and pupils are essentially simple and traversable – must be answered by a different, wider, more spacious vocabulary, not a new vocabulary but an old-and-new one: that of the Conversation.

I have one final image to present. Like much of what I have cited, it is capable of a good deal of interpretation (= is spacious), but it isn't vague. This is the sage Chuang-Tzu, in Thomas Merton's translation, bringing together the motifs of silence, equality, spaciousness and fruitfulness:

> *"The wise man, when he must govern, knows how to do nothing. Letting things alone, he rests in his original nature. Let him keep still, not looking, not hearing. Let him sit like a corpse, with the Dragon power alive all around him. In complete silence his voice will be like thunder … unconcerned, doing nothing, he will see all things grow ripe around him."*

Linking Chris Woodhead to the Dragon Power is perhaps not the kindest way of drawing attention to the inadequacy of some, or many, current and powerful voices in education. But, situated where we are, with the suburbs of dissent gaping, presenting such images is one of the few ways in which our abnormal conditions of debate can be counteracted. Images of this kind are in desperately short supply at the moment, not so much in our imaginations as in the presumed area where 'debate' ought to be happening. That, I think, is the trouble – there's no natural exchange between 'our imaginations' and that area. The space of understanding needs extending; and if that space becomes illimitable, then, as it were, so what? Space *is* illimitable, and so is the Conversation. And so are we.

To the minds that equate liberty of conscience and a hypocrites'charter, such an exchange would no doubt be synonymous with confusion. It would probably take time for us to be able to trust it. But when that had happened, answerings of situations, a kind of sinuous unfolding of realisations, would emerge. I have no idea of what exactly they might be, of course; I, if I were around, would only be one voice in that conversation, and so would you. But I do know that we would be gratifyingly alive and aware within that conversation, and that is the only truly 'realistic' (to use that dishonoured word) arrangement of matters. At the moment we have no realism, only anger, caricature, demolition, and a kind of silly and insecure – but also tragic – showing-off.

So it should be clear that I have no wish to set up counter-images, or ways of thinking which precipitate Conversation, in any simple manner *against* the finalised superstition of the polarity-mongers. I want to be understood by them (and not merely have them 'hear what I'm saying'). Any terminology, including that used here, could be cramped and fetishised and used to deny Conversation, and a good way to do this would be to make it seem as though it *merely confronts* the dazzling and distorting systematism it seeks to be heard by. I am not hoping to erect defences, that is, against some eternal enemy. I do believe, of course, that the *literally* nonsensical attitude against which I'm arguing is something which cannot naturally connect with what we know to be ourselves; all of us know that. It seizes its chance where there is no debate ('Voices'); it encourages us to behave like Punch and Judy ('Schools'); it collapses richness to primitive bigotry ('Magic'); it warps our general understanding ('Spaces'). But it must be engaged with, and we must be optimistic that we can reach those voices and understandings which have been deluded by its promises of safety, certainty, and solutions. The Conversation means, after all, that kindly, liberating, if mysterious, contact with what is not ourselves by which alone we all live.

So - away with Punch and Judy. Let there be the Conversation[53].

Notes

(1) Oakeshott, 'The voice of Poetry in the Conversation of Mankind', in *Rationalism in Politics* (Oxford, 1962)

(2) eg Oliver Sacks, David Cook's *Walter*, the Big Issue, the website, ...

(3) Before long even the Test and County Cricket Board will make a statement about its commitment and grown-upness, and then that'll be the lot.

(4) Similarly, Keats described (in a letter) Sir Charles Dilke, (whose grandson was later to cause a huge Victorian scandal centring on the number of people who ought to be in bed with each other at any one time), as "a man who cannot feel he has a personal identity unless he has made up his mind about everything".

(5) Clichés do, though. Perhaps they are finalised metaphors. For one meaning of 'finalised' as used here, see Bakhtin, *Dostoevsky's Poetics*: "Both relativism and dogmatism exclude all argument, all authentic dialogue, by making it either unnecessary or impossible."

(6) cf Iain McGilchrist, *Against Criticism* (Faber, 1982)

(7) One logical result is that such teachers no longer spend their own money on school supplies - £50, £100 a year? Millions, anyway, overall.

(8) Kim as in *Kim*, Rudyard Kipling

(9) I say "poisonous" because, as I write, the fourth suicide directly related to a school inspection has been reported. (*T.E.S.*, 14 April 2000.) Chris Woodhead, responding to the news, said that Ofsted will continue to exercise rigour and that it is sad that the teacher couldn't accept what the inspectors said about her. In other words, according to him, it's her fault. (And now [January 2001] I have to note the fifth suicide. Each is related to a different aspect of the emotionally multifarious inspection ordeal.

(10) The first of these is so vague, and yet so easily acceded to, that we can call it superstitious; in which case Ludwig von Mises' term, 'scientism', meaning a superstitious faith in popular notions of scientific method, is preferable to 'science').

(11) Malinowski, *Coral Gardens and their Magic* (George Allen & Unwin, 1935)

(12) Similar comments apply to the DfEE's latest 'targets', 20%, 25%, 30% and all that. If the idea were to convince us that these figures are reasonably derived from current trends plus achievable improvements, they'd have read things like 17.2%, 23.6%, 29.4%. Why don't they, then? Because their real purpose is to sing out merrily from newspaper headlines and to be remembered by parents. The kind of parent who would remember a figure like 23.6%, however, might sometimes be the kind of parent sceptical about targets plucked from the air. It's not statistics which is the problem, but the popular image of statistics.

(13) Six weeks after my own school's inspection, I was asked to take over and teach Drama during a neighbouring school's inspection. Their Drama teacher had suddenly retired early (about thirty-five years early). This inspection team had importantly different procedures from the previous one. They told us each morning which lessons would be observed that day, and what a difference that made. They talked to us during the lesson about what was happening, and made notes of what we said. They gave us feedback at the end of each lesson. So where does that leave the superstitious mummery about '98.4% of lessons were satisfactory'? The experimental conditions aren't the same.

(14) Lionel Trilling: "The intellectual life of our culture ... fosters a form of assent which does not involve actual credence" (*Beyond Culture*, Secker & Warburg, 1966)

(15) In *An Outline of Psychoanalysis*, tr. J Strachey (London: Holgarth Press and Institute of Psychoanalysis, 1949)

(16) W La Barre, *The Ghost Dance* (George Allen & Unwin, 1970)

(17) Another might be that we have to do without God. Many people, including myself, don't feel this as a paralysing lack, but it is a lack of a comfort the nineteenth century felt acutely - see Thomas Hardy's extraordinary attempts to accept the melancholy with which it visited him. It's a lack of a comfort we may feel glad to be rid of, but this itself is evidence of the *huge* pressure on people today to be *grown up*. So we disguise regression.

(18) I can't resist quoting more fully from Allport here. He is speaking of a child in a world of menacing giants: "There are a great many things such a dwarf-child may do, all of them serving

as his ego-defences. He may withdraw into himself, speaking little to giants and never honestly. He may band together with other dwarfs, sticking close to them for comfort and self-respect. He may try to cheat the giants when he can, and thus have a taste of sweet revenge. He may in desperation push some giant off the sidewalk or throw a rock at him when it is safe to do so. Or he may out of despair find himself acting the part that the giant expects, and gradually grow to share his master's own uncomplimentary view of dwarfs." (*The Nature of Prejudice*, Doubleday Anchor, 1958) Staffroom defences, all of them. And what happens to the person who once felt dwarf-like, and now, occupying a headteacher's chair or public office, needs to act the part of a genuine, card-carrying giant?

(19) 'Real' or 'really' as an intensifying adverb: late nineteenth century.

(20) Wittgenstein: "The results of philosophy are the uncovering of bumps that the understanding has got by running its head up against the limits of language." (*Philosophical Investigations*, Blackwell, 1953). Use of 'real' as an attempt to avoid bumps, or assuage them?

(21) Somewhere: it is quoted in Guy Debord's *Society of the Spectacle* (1983, Detroit, Mich.)

(22) Wittgenstein, op. cit.

(23) Lasch, *The Minimal Self* (Norton, 1984)

(24) Baudrillard, *The Transparency of Evil* (Verso, 1993)

(25) I'm not that kind of a luddite.

(26) It even hints at a characterisation of mankind: the animal which grants reality to what is not itself.

(27) Trilling's point, in *Sincerity and Authenticity* (O.U.P., 1972)

(28) The 'clutter of effect' I mentioned earlier calls to us in many and confusing ways - to be the kind of person the call (eg an advert) implies, to accord our lifestyle to it, to communicate through it. Such calls may be puny, compared with the calls our grandparents might have heard, but they *seem* to appeal to our *selves*. What can we do with such shallow appeals to our being, not our periphery, except become confused about what and where our being is?

(29) in *Postmodernism* (Verso, 1991)

(30) in *The Changing Nature of Man* (1961)

(31) in *The Meaning of History* (Geoffrey Bles, 1936)

(32) 'Subject/object', in *The Essential Frankfurt School Reader* (Blackwell, 1978). The thing which gets Adorno in trouble with strict Marxists – or used to – is his insistence that there is also no corresponding ultimate *future* unity between subject and object.

(33) Introduction to the English edition, 1954.

(34) .... variety, duality, otherness, mystery, spaciousness, reality ...

(35) Compare Rupert Brooke, 'Peace', where the outbreak of war lets English youth 'turn, as swimmers into cleanness leaping/Glad from a world grown old and cold and weary'.

(36) Oddly, given the usual tendency to think of modern business and industry overvaluing objectivity. But it is part of the meaning of this essay that, often, what seems to be objective is in fact subjective.

(37) According to the *New Scientist*, 12 August 2000, half of the world's 6,800 languages will vanish in two generations.

(38) *Walden*, 1854

(39) Or 'scientist of the diagonal', as he called himself. I just love that. And it is a *spatial metaphor*.

(40) cf Alice Walker, *The Universe Responds*, 1987: the existence of free animal life is 'the spiritual equivalent of oxygen'.

(41) Bakhtin: language as 'dialogical', utterances 'filled with echoes and reverberations', voices 'interanimate' and 'populate' each other (*The Dialogic Image*, 1981). Harold Bloom: poems as 'about', in the end, other poems and the spaces they occupy (*The Anxiety of Influence*, 1973)

(42) *The Human Condition* (Chicago University Press, 1958)

(43) BBC 2, 26 April 1995. Cf A S Neill, *Autobiography*: 'I discovered nothing … if I have any special talent it is that of staying in the background'.

(44) Letter to George & Thomas Keats, 22 December, 1817.

(45) Coleridge: poetry is "the touch of a blind man, feeling the face of a darling child" (letter to Southey, 13 July, 1802). Tact, yes. And images of touch as against vision(s) is a promising area for a thesis.

(46) Sometimes, though words aren't defined as synonyms, they are used as if saying the one is enough to imply the other: as 'outmoding' and 'resolution', in the 'Voices' section.

(47) Do Macmillan nurses offer solutions to terminally-ill patients? Of course not; not only would it be an absurdity, it would be an impertinence. They answer them. They offer recognition. It still seems to me a miracle that such answering can help, but perhaps one way to characterise it might be to suggest that answering breaks through the sense of ultimate aloneness that anxiety causes. If that is so, in this sense answering creates space, and is valued as such even at the end of one's life.

(48) Perhaps acknowledgement, rather than knowledge, is our greatest gift. If so, it's a very great one.

(49) A great deal of interest in decipherment in the last hundred years: the Baconian controversy, Purple, Enigma, the Bible Code, … Does it reflect this continuing prickling fantasy that the Truth must be out there somewhere?

(50) See Richmal Crompton. No, don't. Footnotes allow for play, it seems to me; they are spacious, in exactly the sense Ernst would shave clean.

(51) *Faking it: the Sentimentalisation of Modern Society* (London: Social Affairs Unit, 1998).

(52) 26 April, 1998.

(53) Michael Oakeshott, who started all this, deserves the last word here.
"The pursuit of learning is not a race in which competitors jockey for first place, nor an argument or a symposium; it is a conversation … it has no predetermined course, we do not ask what it is 'for', and we do not judge its excellence by its conclusions … its integration is not superimposed, but springs from the quality of the voices which speak … A university will have ceased to exist when its learning has degenerated into research, its teaching has become mere instruction, and when those who come to be taught come, not in search of their intellectual fortune, but with a vitality so unroused or exhausted that they wish to be provided with a serviceable moral and intellectual outfit, … a qualification for earning a living, or a certificate to let them in on the exploitation of the world."
(*The Voice of Liberal Learning*, ed Fuller, Yale 1989)

Cultivating Emptiness

When emptiness is possible,
Everything is possible;
Were emptiness impossible,
Nothing would be possible.[1]

Nagarjuna

---

(1) Batchelor, Stephen. Verses from the Center: *a Buddhist Vision of the Sublime.*
New York: Riverhead Books, 2000.

Cultivating Emptiness: Helen Cross

Helen Cross grew up in Scotland. She studied Music and English Literature at Glasgow University and worked for a while in music selling and in the NHS before training as a teacher with Robert Graham at Durham University. Since then she has taught in schools in the North East and South West of England. More recently she has combined this with further study, writing and other activities. She completed an MA in 'Life Writing' at the University of York and is joint author of 'Literature, Criticism and Style,' a popular textbook for A-level students. Currently, she is also an Associate Lecturer for the Open University, is training in psychotherapy, and remains a keen amateur musician.

Playing Jenga

In the hall of the Primary School, my eye was caught by a display of paintings of leaves. I stood for a moment enjoying the variety of shapes and bright colours, then stepped forward for a closer look. Beside each painting was stapled a small, neatly ruled sheet of paper, headed with a child's name and class. A moment's calculation told me that this was the work of children aged around eight. Poems, perhaps? No. Each sheet had on it two headings: 'Self-assessment' and 'Targets', beneath which the children had carefully inscribed statements about their work.

'I made the stalk too long.'
'I should paint inside the outline better.'
'I didn't mix the colours right.'
'I shouldn't of painted it blue.'

I stepped back quickly, but it seemed that all the colour had drained out of the bright leaves.

There is a small incident in a story I used to read with younger school pupils, *The Turbulent Term of Tyke Tyler*, which goes something like this: Tyke has a friend, Danny, who is 'not very bright', and the two of them are in a painting lesson in their last year at Junior School. Danny is busy painting when Tyke asks what his picture is supposed to be.

'A robin,' answers Danny.
'Robins aren't blue!' says Tyke scornfully.

Danny, as I remember it, does not shrivel up or lose heart and say 'I shouldn't of painted it blue,' but retorts cheerfully,

'I like it blue,' and carries on painting.

I have no idea whether the child who wrote 'I shouldn't of painted it blue' and her classmates lost heart, but it seemed to me that their paintings had. I experienced them as becoming colourless and 'empty', because they had not been allowed simply to 'be'. It was as if they had been made less important than they actually were, yet simultaneously had been forced to carry more weight and importance than was actually appropriate. Letting them stand alone would, I suppose, not have been sufficiently 'educational' and their teacher would have felt she had not done her job properly. Something more had to be done - and be seen to be done.

Whether or not the young painters lost heart, they might have begun to learn something about the pattern of things to come in the eight or ten or so years of schooling still ahead of them, not to mention any number of years more of higher education, training, or on the 'pathways' of 'Lifelong Learning'.

For not letting things be and, in the process, emptying the heart out of them, is something we seem to do rather a lot these days.

Recently, after a break of more than a year, I ventured once again into teaching English in a secondary school, which I shall call 'The Chase', since I spent most of my time there chasing my tail and a hunted feeling seemed to be rather a feature of the place. "You have to watch your back here," a colleague warned me on the first morning. I found myself the stand-in teacher to a group who were working on assignments for their GCSE coursework. A few weeks into the job, I was beginning to wonder what I was up to. I had been dipping into a book in which it was suggested that the most important thing we can ask ourselves about what we do is whether 'our path has heart.'

'I find myself engaged in something that feels more and more an empty mechanical process of going through certain motions in order that particular outcomes can be achieved. Targets have to be hit and criteria met, otherwise the writing the students produce - however brilliant it may be - will be invalid and not make the grade. This is a terrible responsibility - a big burden. I don't remember it all being quite so desperately serious in the past. How did it all get so heavy?

'I used to enjoy reading students' responses to literary texts we had studied together. We might have done that absolutely standard exercise of playing with a text like To Kill a Mockingbird by doing exactly what Harper Lee suggests – 'standing in someone else's shoes and walking around in them'[2] a bit, in order to understand a little better not just the plot but the background to it and the perceptions and emotional reactions of the characters, by using role play and empathic writing. The written responses would all have been different. Reading thirty of them, each four or six pages long, was a big task,

but one that could be very moving; or yield a surprise or two, or even make me laugh.

'Now it all feels quite different. We certainly don't 'play' with texts or ideas. If I do not prepare this group adequately for the task, there is a danger that they just may not write 'the right thing'. They might fail to display an explicit - since implicit is not good enough nowadays - understanding of the historical and social backgrounds of these two short stories we have to compare, for example; or in writing about the play they have just read, they might not concentrate all their attention on the dramatist's techniques, but be sidetracked into such irrelevancies as responding to characters and their situations with empathy, or expressing their feelings, and so fail to meet the criteria for the A-C grades I am under pressure to enable them to achieve, since this school is a 'good' school and holds a very respected position in the league tables for examination results, which must be maintained at all costs. There is a '2 + 2' system, as well, which means that we are expected to 'add' two National Curriculum levels to pupils' performance between their arrival at the school and their Key Stage 3 tests and two more between Key Stage 3 and Key Stage 4.

'Therefore, I create special worksheets so that they can collect only the 'right' information about those two stories and then give them a paragraph-by-paragraph guide so that they can write the 'correct' essay. The same with the play - Priestley's An Inspector Calls. No more Eva Smith's Diary, even for the least academic members of this class. No more empathy. No more even getting into what the play is really about, it seems. Too political, perhaps? More, that there just isn't time for all that. I've got to make sure they demonstrate their understanding of dramatic irony and the Classical Unities.

'All the assignments come out more or less the same apart from variations in how well they're written. No emotional responses, no surprises and certainly no laughter. Reading them and annotating them is very time-consuming, but would be merely boring if I were not so anxious about whether they are up to standard. In class, I am becoming rigid and humourless. I'm not surprised that most of the class are not very interested in literature. Probably they are starting to feel like the pupils in Doctor Blimber's academy in Dickens's Dombey and Son, who

"at the end of the first twelvemonth had arrived at the conclusion, from which [they] never afterwards departed, that all the fancies of the poets, and lessons of the sages, were a mere collection of words and grammar, and had no other meaning in the world.'

Perhaps these sound like the words of someone who begrudges time spent reading and responding to her pupils' work - someone disillusioned, or work-shy. In accepted terms, it is probably true. A head of English told me the other day that when some of the less experienced teachers in her department complained about their workload, she had wanted to tell them to just get on with it - *"That's the way the cookie crumbles, nowadays,"* she said. (Once, I was a member of a school's 'Working Party on Workload' - a group which was convened twice before being dissolved because everybody was far too busy to attend the meetings.)

Workload in itself was not quite where the problem lay, however. It was more a sense that I was conscientiously devoting around twelve hours a day to something which felt *empty*, and rather desperately following a path with not very much heart at all. Some lines from Oscar Wilde seemed all too apt:

> *We live in the age of the over-worked, and the under-educated; the age in which people are so industrious that they become absolutely stupid* [3]

And (though not quite with his intentions)

> *To be good, according to the vulgar standard of goodness, is obviously quite easy. It merely requires a certain amount of sordid terror, a certain lack of imaginative thought, and a certain low passion for middle-class respectability* [4].

'Being good', and terribly 'industrious', I felt myself on some level to be becoming increasingly 'stupid'. Yet when we are part of it all, on the inside, and so subject to 'sordid terror', it seems absolutely necessary to 'watch our backs', maintain at least the appearance of 'respectability' and keep trying to do just what is expected.

And what seems to be expected is this 'hole-in-the-heart' education, in which we teach, and assess pupils' grasp of the 'structure' and 'techniques' of literature, and don't have any time left for 'the fancies of the poets', the 'lessons of the sages', or what it might actually be all about.

Considering what Priestley's 'Inspector' has to say about the potentially catastrophic consequences of remaining blind to the ways in which our actions may affect others, and Harper Lee's exhortation to step 'into other peoples' shoes and walk around in them', I suspect many such writers would have laughed like drains to find that responding to their work with empathy is no longer considered sufficiently 'educational' to meet the requirements for literary study for fifteen year-olds.

The Buddhist scholar, Stephen Batchelor, suggests an 'ethics of empathy' which comes about through *moments when we experience ourselves not at odds with others but as participants in a shared reality. As empathic beings in a participatory reality we cannot, without losing our integrity, hurt, abuse, rob, or lie to others.*

Ethical integrity originates in empathy, for then we take the well-being of others to heart...[5]

That is an idea I'd like to return to later, but for now, I'll content myself with asking whether broadening the scope of our 'shared reality' isn't one of the chief motives for reading, teaching or studying literature and the other arts? And how, other than by practising empathy, can we begin to get a real sense of what is right and wrong in our dealings with other people, as opposed to merely complying with moral codes? How else can we develop the capacity for compassion? And much more than the quality of our individual day to day interactions may hinge on the human capacity for compassion. Yet we don't seem able to allow this to 'just be' at the heart of what we do.

There is a game called 'Jenga', popular with children and adults, which begins with a lot of small wooden bricks stacked into a compact, stable tower. Players take it in turns to remove bricks, by sliding them carefully out of the lower levels, and then add them to the top, while trying not to demolish the whole thing. Gradually, as it gets higher, the structure becomes more and more hollow at the base and more and more precarious. Eventually, someone is forced to attempt the impossible, topples the tower, sends bricks flying in all directions, and pays a forfeit.

We sometimes seem to be playing a special, educational version of Jenga, as we carefully pull the heart out of our endeavours and try to balance it somewhere else. Once we have extricated the potentially ethics-building empathy-brick from its place at the heart of things, for example, the resulting emptiness begins to have consequences, so we do two things. Concerned about 'falling moral standards,' we decide that ethics needs to be taught, so we stick some on top of the stack somewhere, in the form of 'citizenship' or 'moral education' classes, where, not properly connected or grounded, it is so wobbly that no-one trusts it or takes it seriously. Then, because the tower is beginning to sway rather dangerously, we panic a bit about academic standards and change the rules of the game. We try to shore up the shaky structure: we begin to plug the gaps, stuffing educational polyfilla - dramatic techniques, endless assessments, criteria and targets, form-filling and box-ticking - into all the spaces, ensuring that there will be no room left anyway, should that vital brick ever threaten to slip back down into its place.

And this 'hole-in-the-heart' education is getting above itself. We don't just apply this principle to literature, art, or other 'curriculum areas' but to life itself.

In the last few years, all post-16 students have begun to be assessed not just for academic ability or vocational training, but for their 'Key Skills', such as *'Improving Own Learning and Performance'* and *'Problem Solving.'* Despite all appearances to the contrary in the form of abundant multi-paged documents detailing 'portfolio evidence requirements,' these 'Key Skills' are supposed to be integral to any programme of study. It's just that now they need to be 'evidenced'. So we add yet another very dodgy brick in the form of special lessons for the creation of 'evidence portfolios'.

Only this week, some conscientious visiting German students expressed what seemed to me an entirely proper reaction to *'Improving own Learning and Performance'*:

"But we know how to study," they said in genuine bewilderment, obviously a little affronted that simply getting on with learning, performing - and, incidentally, improving by leaps and bounds - was not enough in itself and that something more, in the form of a specially concocted task, had to be done in order to 'evidence' this.

As for *'Problem-solving'*, these are not, of course, the sort of 'problems' we used to tackle, when I was at school, in Maths, or like the ones which foxed me in Physics, never my strongest subject:

If a polar bear of mass x kg, wearing a bullet-proof vest and sitting (friction compensated) on an ice-floe, is shot by a hunter with a bullet of mass y kg, which travels at z m/s, at what speed will the bear move off across the ice when it is struck by the bullet?

I always thought it would scarper pretty fast, but that was not the point. No, these are supposed to be 'real-life' problems and we are expected to find ways to assess peoples' ability to solve them.

What if a student is actually facing a real-life problem, though, like Ben, a young man I taught at 'The Chase'? Ben's mother had died during the summer before he began his A-level course, his father had left years before, and in order to go on with his studies, he had to lodge with an aunt, who while she was sympathetic enough, could not undertake to look after him. A lot of his energy went into simply coping, which he appeared to do quite admirably. It was also quite apparent that he would not be able to provide the 'evidence requirements' for *'Problem Solving'* or *'Improving Own Learning and Performance'*. He was an able student, read and participated with enthusiasm, got involved with literature, learned all his lines and was a comic hit in the class production of *The Importance of being Earnest*. Written work defeated him, though. It was not that he *couldn't* write essays, he just *didn't*. He was quite honest about the fact that at home, all his problem-solving energy went into organising his life - getting himself out of bed and to school and preparing his own meals - and there wasn't enough left over for homework. He knew what he could do, and that he could probably pull it off in the exams and get a decent grade. (He did.) His approach seemed pretty grown up and balanced, all things considered. His problem-solving ability was surely more than adequate and very *appropriate*, but how could we begin - or presume - to assess it, or worse still, provide 'evidence' for it?

No, in order to assess *'problem-solving'*, we have, once again, to add something. Problems, in other words. We have to manufacture them specially, so that candidates can

'produce evidence to demonstrate their skills in Problem Solving in some or all of the following areas:

1. Explore a complex problem, come up with **three** options for solving it and justify the option selected for taking it forward.

2. Plan and implement at least **one** option for solving the problem, review progress and revise approach as necessary.

3. Apply agreed methods to check if the problem has been solved, describe the results and review approach to problem solving.

But what is really going on here? In the name of giving students more responsibility for their own learning, we just take away more of their living space, fill it with educational polyfilla, in the form of the 'Key Skills' lesson, and in fact try to take on some of the responsibility, which is *actually* theirs already, for how they run their lives as students. In order to assess their 'Key Skills', we have to pull another basic brick out of the middle and stick it in a wobbly and untrustworthy position on the top. In other words, we *invent* problems for them to solve, so we can tick the relevant 'problem-solving' skills boxes, and devise artificial ways for them to set themselves targets, agree objectives, 'establish cooperative relationships' and so on, leaving them less time and space for doing the real thing. The processes we go through up on top somewhere will just become more and more unreal, irrelevant and empty. Instead of bringing education closer to 'real life', which is presumably what the intention is here, we actually make it more remote.

At the same time, we are also, surely, going to create, for ourselves and the students, some serious confusion about motivation. Do we do things because they are intrinsically 'real' and worthwhile, or merely in order to 'evidence' something?

Back at 'The Chase', forms were distributed to enable teachers to apply for a new Performance Related Pay scheme. At first, quite a lot of people stalked around, barely disguising their hurt and outrage behind declarations that they would on no account fill them in.

> *"I don't exactly earn a fortune, but it's enough to get by on. If I have to fill that in, then they can keep their two thousand pounds, thanks very much."*

> *"If what I do's not good enough, then tough! I'm already working as hard as I possibly can."*

On the whole, I was pretty relieved that, being on a temporary contract, I didn't qualify to go through this process, despite doom-laden remarks to the effect that getting jobs would be impossible if one hadn't met the requirements for 'crossing the threshold' – or to be more exact, couldn't provide 'evidence' that one had done so.

And for crossing that 'threshold', all sorts of evidence would be required and not just examination results and 'add-on' values like the 2+2 system, either.

Along with the forms, there came leaflets and handouts and meetings offering advice on how to approach filling them in, or in other words, on how the evidence should be presented in order to bring about the desired result. Among other things, it was suggested that one should keep some sort of log-book, in which to record every activity that might contribute to meeting all these 'evidence requirements'. Under 'Pastoral Care', for example, you might make a note each time you had dealings with a pupil. Perhaps it would be something like this:

I remember the time when a quiet lad, called Michael, from a rather difficult year 9 group, sought me out one break time, when I was on duty outside, to tell me how upset he was about the recent death of his grandfather, and how he couldn't talk to anyone at home because his father was away and his mother wasn't coping very well, and he was afraid of his form tutor. He talked to me for a few minutes and I paid attention. I think I tentatively suggested that he could write something about his grandfather next time we were writing something in an English lesson, if he felt like it. I think he did. A minor incident – one of those rare moments when it feels quite all right to be the sort of teacher people are not afraid of.

Now, though, like blue leaves, such moments cannot be allowed to just be. Had I been busy collecting evidence for my threshold application, I would, of course, have rushed triumphantly to get my log-book so that I could write *'Consulted by pupil on personal matter. Used counselling skills (and by the way, don't forget I've been doing a course in that at* **weekends***, because I'm so dedicated to professional development!')* Perhaps, too, I'd have had to pursue Michael at the next break time, and ask him to sign my log-book, just to consolidate that 'evidence'. Once again, something small but precious would have been diminished, or demeaned, while also being burdened with an inappropriate weight.

I got to know Michael a little better sometime later when we spent a weekend in the Lake District with the school's Rambling Club. Had the log-book been about, I suppose that when it turned cold on top of Helvellyn and I lent my spare jumper to one of his friends and my hat to another, he might well have expected me to whip it out of my rucksack to record this self-sacrificing piece of pastoral care and collect more signatures, instead of sharing a joke about just how many garments I might be prepared to part with.

Remembering those small happenings, I notice quite a sense of loss. Such moments hardly ever seem to happen now. It was obviously quite a few years ago, in the days when it was still possible to allow pupils to write things to which we didn't have to apply national curriculum levels; to write things simply because there was something to say. I know, too, that it couldn't have happened recently, because I am fairly sure that in 'The Chase', I would not have been standing still long enough to exchange more than a superficial 'Hi' with any pupil in any break time. I'm fairly sure, too, that I would have been giving off warning signals carrying the message, 'just don't ask me for anything – I haven't time and I couldn't concentrate on what you are saying anyway because I'm too busy watching my back.'

Some pop-psychologist or other turned the word responsibility into 'response-ability', or, the ability to respond, but there seems to be precious little space left, now, for anyone to be able to respond to anything much at all, whether it is a pupil being allowed room to simply respond to literature, or a busy teacher being able to stop watching her back and turn round for long enough to attend, just for a minute or two, to a pupil's confidence. To be able to respond, we require at least a modicum of trust, and enough space to turn round. But shoring up shaky structures with educational polyfilla doesn't leave room to breathe, or to be.

Perhaps, then, this empty education is not really empty at all, but over-full. In our stupid industriousness, we are so busy trying to plug any gap in which anything might happen spontaneously - which might, of course, involve mistakes, failures, things which just don't quite work, or worst of all, things which are not assessable - that there's hardly even a 'hole in the heart' left. Instead, the chambers and arteries are so clogged with 'polyfilla' that the heart is simply stifled and may give up trying altogether. Perhaps a bit of emptiness is not such a bad thing after all.

Making Room for Mystery

Emptiness, it seems, looks like something different, depending on your point of view. I began by using the word negatively, to suggest a lack of something. I was trying to put into words a sense that rather a lot of the activity I and others were engaged in seemed hollow, heart-less, or devoid of some important quality that would make it meaningful. After some exploration, emptiness became instead a vital space, giving room to breathe, to turn round, and to respond. In a sense, it is emptiness itself which allows our activities to have that quality of being truly meaningful. 'Meaning' is of course a slippery, subjective customer. What seems meaningful to me may not necessarily be so to anyone else, but I shall let the word stand, for lack of any obvious alternative.

Whichever way we look at emptiness, it can seem a frightening thing. If we allow ourselves to contemplate it, we may not be able to avoid seeing what's really going on. If our activities are empty because they lack some quality which seems crucial, and if we allow ourselves enough empty space to breathe and turn round, we may catch a glimpse of what we have lost amidst the sheer busy-ness of our frantic efforts to build ever higher, more hollow towers and then to assuage our anxiety about their instability by stuffing them with polyfilla. And what happens if we should happen to encounter, even just momentarily, another kind of 'Emptiness', one which reveals that all sorts of things we take for granted, even our 'selves', are nothing more than a collection of concepts, and which allows us to sense instead the interconnectedness of all things? We may catch a whiff of mystery that could change our perspective irrevocably.

Perhaps it was because, on some level, I sensed that my own life, not just my work, felt a bit like an over-full, shored up, but shaky, 'jenga' structure, and that my relationship with space and emptiness needed investigating, that I was drawn, a year or so ago, to spend some time at a Rural Retreat Centre, where time is divided between outdoor work on the land, other tasks required to sustain the life of a small community, and periods of meditation. The idea of 'retreating temporarily from the world at large' to live in beautiful surroundings, in a 'contemplative atmosphere', for a while, attracted me.

My first evening on retreat just happened to coincide with a talk on Education at the nearby non-denominational Buddhist College to which the retreat centre is affiliated. Out of the silence, the teacher, who had joined us in sitting cross-legged on the floor, began to talk quietly. Education, he explained, has no real equivalent in Buddhist culture. The nearest word in Pali, the language of the oldest Indian Buddhist writings, is *Bhavana*, which means 'cultivation', 'development', or 'bringing into being'. The idea is to bring into being, through practices like meditation, states of mind which may make possible a degree of insight into the nature of life and the human condition, and in so doing, to cultivate wisdom and compassion.

Insight, wisdom and compassion. Those sounded like good things to me, but in my experience, such words don't tend to be heard much, these days, in the world of education.

And cultivation. What would that mean, exactly? At the retreat centre, we did quite a lot of it, in its more usual sense, in the organic vegetable garden. It involves digging and turning the soil over, to aerate it; if necessary, we enrich it with compost, the broken down, fermented growth of past years; we create the conditions in which seeds can germinate and develop. After we've put the seeds in at the right depth, we stand back and give the small plants the time and space they need in order to grow. It is a process which requires faith and which cannot be hurried. It's no use digging up seedlings every few days to see if their growth is 'on target'. Some of my experiences in schools like The Chase, however, seemed more reminiscent of the kind of metaphorical 'cultivation' offered at Doctor Blimber's establishment, in Dickens's *Dombey and Son*, which produced the disaffected pupils mentioned earlier. It was

> *a great hothouse, in which there was a forcing apparatus incessantly at work. All the boys blew before their time. Mental green-peas were produced at Christmas, and intellectual asparagus all the year round. Mathematical gooseberries (very sour ones too) were common at untimely seasons, and from mere sprouts of bushes, under Doctor Blimber's cultivation. Every description of Greek and Latin vegetable was got off the driest twigs of boys, under the frostiest circumstances. Nature was of no consequence at all. No matter what a young gentleman was intended to bear, Doctor Blimber made him bear to pattern, somehow or other.*

> *This was all very pleasant and ingenious, but the system of forcing was attended with its usual disadvantages. There was not the right taste about the premature productions, and they didn't keep well.*

Back at the talk, the speaker went on to explain that in some traditions, young Buddhist monks spend many hours, for many years, simply reciting scriptures and learning verses by heart. Apart from the fact that the intention behind it was 'spiritual', it didn't sound so very different from the rote-learning and repetition we associate with Victorian schoolrooms or the sort of thing my uncle, headmaster of a rural primary school, used to do more recently, when he made the whole school recite their multiplication tables in a sort of rhythmic chant; the sort of thing, indeed, of which we may tend to be rather critical now. It doesn't sound very creative; isn't it rather mechanical, empty, even?

Yet perhaps there is a difference between the ways, in which such activities were approached and some of the 'polyfilla'-tasks and busy-ness we seem so determined to engage in nowadays. Reciting multiplication tables until they were ingrained in the memory, so that figures could be recalled instantly, when required for some purpose, for the remainder of a person's life, was a useful *practice* before the invention of calculators. (My father, who began work as a messenger for the Admiralty at 14 and went on to become a customs officer, was used to performing long complicated feats of mental arithmetic all his life, and could still, at the age of eighty, easily outpace my fumbling efforts with the calculator.) The young Buddhist monks also recite their hundreds of verses as a *practice*. This is part of the 'cultivation' - the tilling of the soil and creation of conditions - that may enable the growth of insight, wisdom and compassion. Practice is preliminary and necessary, but it is not quite the same as the thing itself, though it may be part of it, and may never be finite. Practice is not really an end in itself, but something which opens up possibilities or spaces in which something 'meaningful' can arise. In English teaching, we sometimes ask pupils to do grammar practice exercises, constructing sentences according to the correct pattern, but this is only worthwhile if 'transfer' takes place - if they can then make use of the pattern to express meanings of their own. It doesn't always work, by any means. Practices like meditation or the repeated chanting of verses are a bit like this, or like the scales and arpeggios of a pianist, which once they become ingrained, or habitual, provide the freedom which enables the pianist to play and interpret music. 'Spiritual' practices are undertaken in the hope of gradually developing a more open, spacious view of things and greater freedom of interpretation in relation to life itself.

This kind of cultivation differs radically from what seems to be going on in the world of education these days. It is like planting an unknown seed and waiting patiently to see what plant might grow and emerge. We have to continue to nurture it, to provide it with water and air, to make sure it has enough space and is not choked by weeds, even though we have no idea, really, what 'it' is going to be, and then once we've done that work, we have to stand back and allow growth to take place in its own way. Maybe we hope, or have faith, that cultivation and practice will bear certain kinds of fruit, but we can't demand precise, measurable results. We have to be content with not knowing; we have to be prepared to accept, or even welcome, mystery.

In so much of education, though, the trend *is* towards a demand for measurable results. A friend of mine, a respected University professor of Physics, was lost for words, recently, because she had been informed by an administrator that she must on no account use the word 'understanding' in her department's policy documents. Developing students' understanding of the principles of Physics was not allowed to be one of her aims, because, she was told, it is not possible to measure 'understanding' numerically. Did this mean that all she had been aiming to do for the past fifteen years was no longer valid?

And my neighbour has just been telling me about those 'literacy hours' in which she can no longer simply read stories or other books with her class of six-year-olds (yes, six-year-olds) for them to be thrilled by, or to laugh at, or to wonder at, but must first engage them in an up to date form of chanting:

"What sort of book is this?"
"This is a fiction book."
"This is a fiction book."

or

"This is a fact book."
"This is a fact book."
"Its genre is........."
"Its genre is.........."
"The author is.........."
"The author wrote x other books."
"The titles are............"

and so on, until there is hardly any time left for the story itself. When these children come to take national tests in literacy the following year, it is their ability to respond to well-rehearsed prompts like these which is measured and which is cited as evidence of rising - or falling - standards.

Why does this kind of chanting seem so much less acceptable than the old-fashioned kind? People were tested on their multiplication tables, after all. *This* kind of rote-learning is not *practice*, however. It has no transfer value - no practical application. It is not even seen as practice either. This *is* 'literacy'. This *is* 'education.' Standards are measured by it. Surely it must be the real thing! But it is not. It is hole-in-the-heart stuff, polyfilla, stifling the spaces where wonder or a sense of mystery might have room to germinate.

It begins to seem that what we are trying to do more and more is to rule out mystery. We seem determined not to leave room for it, and what mystery needs more than anything is space - enough space for it to arise naturally and make its presence felt - and a little bit of cultivation. To get once more in contact with mystery, we may have to stop for a while, wait for a bit, and leave some space, resisting the temptation to push in a bit of polyfilla here or there, and allow ourselves to become more aware of what is in those spaces at the heart of things.

To begin the practice of meditation - to contemplate our being as an experience, from the inside, as it were, not to think about it, but to get a physical, felt sense of it, to become aware of our 'creatureliness', our breathing, our beating hearts, and of how we fit into the world around us - is, almost inevitably, I think, to be struck with amazement at the sheer mysteriousness of almost everything we tend to take for granted. This may of course be blindingly obvious to the reader, but it wasn't, to me, - or at least not more than fleetingly, now and again - and I don't think it is generally. It just isn't something much encouraged in contemporary life.

To rest our attention on something as apparently simple as breathing, for example, is to bring into our awareness, too, our inability to control life and our inter-dependence with all that is around us. We cannot voluntarily stop breathing - or not for long, anyway; neither can we start breathing again once it has stopped, yet a very small change in the atmosphere could make it impossible very quickly. The heartbeat, on which life also depends entirely, is even more remote from control. Life is something precious and vulnerable, which could end at any moment. This awareness, it seems to me, cannot but lead to an overwhelming sense of mystery, to a huge question, like one posed by Zen masters for their students to ponder: 'What is this?' Who am I? What am I? What on earth is this thing called life anyway? Such questions are steps on the path which is sometimes called 'Awakening', a process of becoming mindful 'of what we are – of what our situation truly is,' as the Vietnamese teacher Thich Nhat Hanh puts it.

What we are likely to catch glimpses of, if we question in this way, is 'Emptiness'.

Emptiness is, I suppose, what I encountered momentarily when, one day nearly twenty years ago, I glanced out of the window of a friend's house in Oxford. Afterwards, I wrote:

> Not even a moment, but the tiniest fragment of a moment, a minute inkling in which it is as though all is woven into the most fine and delicate of fabrics, bound all together by the faintest strands of silver, silken thread, sparkling, taut, but gentler than spiders' webbing. All is connected, but in no solid way. A drop of water, about to fall from the edge of the sill hangs and dances in the sunlight; and yet that same silver thread shimmers all through the stolid red

bricks of the terraced houses, the silhouettes of the wintry trees, the blue translucent sky and the peeling paint of the warm window frame under my hand. Desperately fragile, the silver thread is magic, permeating everything, but so tender and fine that it seems one breath could waft it away; so brittle that the breaking of one tiny atom could shatter it all.

As Stephen Batchelor suggests in his introduction to some of the writings of Nagarjuna, the 2nd century poet and thinker whose verse I chose, perhaps a little irreverently, to head these chapters,

Emptiness is a way of talking about the sublime depth, mystery and contingency that are revealed as one probes beneath the surface of anything that seems to exist in self-sufficient isolation. Emptiness is the untraceability of any such isolated thing. Yet for something to be empty does not imply that there is nothing there at all... [6]

Nagarjuna specialised in trying to convey the ungraspable, paradoxical nature of Emptiness, not by writing *about* it, but by trying to *disclose* it from within, 'through the play of language'. It's one of those things that are impossible to pin down, like something you're aware of out of the corner of your eye which vanishes if you turn your full gaze on it. The very attempt to apply rational thought to it whisks it out of reach.

Elsewhere, in a chapter exploring 'Questioning', Batchelor suggests that there are two quite different ways of asking questions. The first kind of questioning is that which is applied to 'problems'. It has recourse to 'the ever-growing quantity of knowledge that has been collected and stored by others', involves the application of reason, practical skill, deduction and calculation, and is very useful in its place. Terming this the 'calculative' approach to questioning, he quotes from Heidegger:

Calculative thinking computes. It computes ever new, ever more promising and at the same time more economical possibilities. Calculative thinking races from one prospect to the next. Calculative thinking never stops, never collects itself

before going on to express his concern that this is becoming ever more pervasive and dominant in contemporary life and that "instead of being merely one faculty among others, it casts its shadow over nearly all areas of human activity."

A calculative attitude tends to be manipulative. It treats life as though it were composed of a virtually infinite number of separate parts. This attitude not only operates in the material realm; it affects our vision of other people and even ourselves. It fragments and divides; it turns living creatures into things. To be able to calculate effectively, we must be able to measure our objects with the exactness and precision demanded by the final aim of successfully manipulating them. To control the diverse elements of reality requires that we see them as separate units capable of being dissected and accumulated, of being rejected and attained.

...calculation...is a useful tool. But it becomes decidedly dangerous when it becomes our predominant attitude towards life as a whole. If our view of the future as well as our ethical decisions are determined only by a calculative attitude, then we are truly in danger of losing altogether our uncertain hold on the threads of a calmer, more contemplative relationship to life. [7]

Calculative questioning is all right in its place, then, but while it may enable us to find solutions to some of our problems, it is 'helpless in penetrating our mysteries'. Problems and mysteries are two very different things:

Unlike a problem, a mystery can never be solved. A mystery can only be penetrated. A problem once solved, ceases to be a problem; but the penetration of a mystery does not make it any less mysterious... The more pervasive is calculation in our lives, the more is the mysterious banished...But the mysterious lies at the heart of our lives, not at the periphery. [8]

An entirely different kind of questioning and a different attitude are required if we are to even contemplate, never mind penetrate, our mysteries. This is, to return to Heidegger, the 'meditative thinking which contemplates the meaning that reigns in everything that is.'

Things don't seem to have changed much since Dickens was warning us, in *Hard Times*, of the consequences we can expect if we allow the calculative approach to dominate our lives. After setting before us his famous, fact-ridden, Gradgrind schoolroom, and his hellish vision of life in the utilitarian factory-scape of Coketown, Dickens leaps out, like an impatient magic lantern projectionist, from behind the picture, to harangue us, just in case we have not got the point, or heard his 'keynote' correctly:

It is known, to the force of a single pound weight, what the engine will do; but, not all the calculators of the National Debt can tell me the capacity for good or evil, for love or hatred, for patriotism or discontent, for the decomposition of virtue into vice, or the reverse, at any single moment in the soul of one of these its quiet servants, with the composed faces and the regulated actions. There is no mystery in it; there is an unfathomable mystery in the meanest of them, for ever. - Supposing we were to reserve our arithmetic for material objects, and to govern these awful unknown quantities by other means!

'Unknown quantities' call for an approach which is meditative rather than calculative; 'unfathomable mystery' needs to be recognised as that in which we live, move and have our being – though a truly meditative attitude might also recognise mystery in those machines, as well as in the people, and be filled with wonder at the whole strange picture.

The real trouble with schoolrooms like those of Blimber and Gradgrind - with the whole utilitarian, Gradgrind culture, is not just that it is dominated by calculation, but that the exaltation of fact into 'the one thing needful' is balanced by an even more sinister prohibition: 'Never wonder.'

> *Herein lay the spring of the mechanical art ...of educating the reason without stooping to the cultivation of the sentiments and affections. Never wonder. By means of addition, subtraction, multiplication and division, settle everything somehow, and never wonder.*

Wonder is forbidden, in the world of Hard Times, or at least firmly discouraged, not least by the circumstance that the unfortunate Coketown factory workers, who put in fifteen hours a day at their machines, and the pupils in M'Choakumchild's or Blimber's classrooms, are simply not left with sufficient time or space to be able to explore it. Of course Dickens is at pains to remind us that it is impossible to stamp - or grind - out the human propensity to wonder entirely, but his warning is that where it is cramped or distorted, people are definitely damaged and hurt.

Poor Louisa Gradgrind, whose imagination has been reduced to a 'fire with nothing to burn' and whose gazing at the 'red sparks dropping out of the fire, and whitening and dying' encourages her to contemplate the shortness and transience of her life, has 'such unmanageable thoughts...that they will wonder.' Her mother, usually inert, is roused to a furious, terrified denial - a denunciation of Louisa's efforts to awaken to the mystery at the heart of life. 'Nonsense!' she cuts her off sharply.

Mystery is just too much for Mrs Gradgrind to cope with, and certainly, as she points out so frequently, were she to encourage Louisa in her meditative questioning, she would 'never hear the last of it' from her husband.

It makes us anxious too, so

> *...we make our lives so hectic that we eliminate the slightest risk of looking into ourselves... In a world dedicated to distraction, silence and stillness*

*terrify us; we protect ourselves from them with noise and frantic busyness.
Looking into the nature of our mind is the last thing we would dare to do.*[9]

For mystery is not comfortable or comforting. It forces us to recognise that there
are things which are unpredictable; far beyond us; things we cannot understand
and control by pinning down, quantifying or labelling. It reminds us that our vision
is a very limited one. It puts us in our place – our proper place. *This* is seeing things
as they are – 'what our situation truly is.' If we don't leave room for a little of this
kind of awareness, how can we begin to recognise that it is possible to have a
wider perspective than the one we generally acknowledge? How can we come to
see that we all share this inevitable state of 'unknowing'? And it seems that it is only
through coming to this sort of realisation that we can develop genuine
compassion and a true respect for ourselves, others and the world which we
inhabit.

It is by no means an unusual idea to make the connection between learning to see
a wider and clearer view of things and developing the capacity for wisdom and
compassion. Many people have done so in different contexts. Perhaps, for
example, Iris Murdoch is saying something a bit like this when she talks about
'good art - especially literature and painting' - in her essay *The sovereignty of good
over other concepts'*:

> *Good art reveals what we are usually too selfish and too timid to recognise, the
> minute and absolutely random detail of the world, and reveals it together with a
> sense of unity and form. This form often seems to us mysterious because it
> resists the easy patterns of the fantasy, whereas there is nothing mysterious
> about the forms of bad art since they are the recognisable and familiar ratruns
> of selfish day-dream. Good art shows us how difficult it is to be objective by
> showing us how differently the world looks to an objective vision. We are
> presented with a truthful image of the human condition in a form which can be
> steadily contemplated; and indeed this is the only context in which many of us
> are capable of contemplating it at all. Art transcends selfish and obsessive
> limitations of personality and can enlarge the sensibility of its consumer. It is a
> kind of goodness by proxy. Most of all it exhibits to us the connection, in* **human**
> *beings, of clear realistic vision with compassion. The realism of a great artist is
> not a photographic realism, it is essentially both pity and justice.*[10]

And Milton seems to be saying something similar in his essay *Of Education*.
The schedule for learning he offers seems preposterous nowadays, for ordinary
mortals, and is perhaps a little too Blimberesque for comfort, but one point he
makes quite clearly is that the true purpose of education is to make us more
like God:

> *'...the end...of learning...is regaining to know God aright and out of that knowledge to love him, to imitate him, to be like him, as we may the neerest by possessing our souls of true vertue, which being united to the heavenly grace of faith makes up the highest perfection. But...our understanding cannot in this body found it self but on sensible things, nor arrive so clearly to the knowledge of God and things invisible, as by orderly conning over the visible and inferior creature...'[11]*

He is not, of course, proposing anything so presumptuous as that we should attempt to make ourselves God's equals or to aspire to God's power. He made that point forcefully enough in *Paradise Lost*. What he does intend, though, is that by immersing themselves in all the languages, sciences, practical skills, arts and literature under the sun, and by a thorough examination of 'the visible and inferior creature', his students should become 'fraught with an universal insight into things.' 'Regaining to know God aright.' The implication is that we are prone to losing sight of our true place in the scheme of things - our sense of 'what our situation truly is,' perhaps - and that education, undertaken in the right spirit, might help restore this to us by enabling us to get a little closer to 'an universal insight' – a 'God's-eye view' of things, in other words. Only then, he suggests, should people be entrusted with positions of responsibility which give them power to make a difference to the lives of others. Since we all have at least a little of that sort of power, we could all do with leaving a bit of room for this kind of 'education'.

I am not about to advocate the introduction of meditation in educational institutions, even though it has been found to be beneficial, in cases where the experiment has been tried; nor am I going to suggest that we should start teaching people modules of mystery, or running courses in compassion, or workshops in wonder. I am sure it would be all too easy for denatured versions of the realms of 'fancy' or the 'sentiments and affections' to be packaged and delivered, devoid of mystery, in neatly presented curriculum units. My point is just the opposite. These are the things which that calculative, 'hole in the heart' 'education' business must leave alone. They are endangered species; their habitat is emptiness - that breathing space which might allow wonder and the appreciation of 'Emptiness' to be brought into being. That threatened habitat needs some careful cultivation, or at the very least, protection from being entirely filled in with 'polyfilla' masquerading as the real thing.

Otherwise, if we go on filling in those spaces too assiduously, is it not likely that we will end up learning our lesson the hard way, like poor old Gradgrind? He realises too late the damage done to his children by their entirely calculative education, and when, in a crisis calling for a compassionate response, he appeals to his all-too-well-trained former pupil, Bitzer, for help, he finds that the model pupil can only respond with the model answer. He pleads,

'Have you a heart?'
'The circulation, sir,' returned Bitzer, smiling at the oddity of the question, 'couldn't be carried on without one. No man, sir, acquainted with the facts established by Harvey relating to the circulation of the blood can doubt that I have a heart.'
'Is it accessible,' cried Mr. Gradgrind, 'to any compassionate influence?'
'It is accessible to Reason, sir,' returned the excellent young man. 'And to nothing else.'

Notes

(1) Batchelor, Stephen. Verses from the Center: a Buddhist Vision of the Sublime. New York: Riverhead Books, 2000.

(2) Lee, Harper. *To Kill a Mockingbird*. London: Heinemann Educational Books, 1960; repr.1985.

(3) Wilde, Oscar. *The Critic as Artist*. Kobenhavn: Green Integer, 1997. p.109.

(4) Ibid. p.154.

(5) Batchelor, Stephen. *Buddhism Without Beliefs: a Contemporary Guide to Awakening*. London: Bloomsbury, 1997. p.46.

(6) Batchelor, Stephen. *Verses from the Center*. p.21

(7) Batchelor, Stephen. *The Faith to Doubt: Glimpses of Buddhist Uncertainty*. Berkeley: Parallax Press, 1990. p.39.

(8) Ibid. p.40.

(9) Sogyal Rinpoche. *The Tibetan book of Living and Dying*. London: Rider, 1992.

(10) Murdoch, Iris. *Existentialists and Mystics: Writings on Philosophy and Literature*. New York: Penguin Books, 1999. p.371.

(11) Milton, John. *Selected Prose*. (Edited by C.A. Patrides). Harmondsworth: Penguin Books, 1974. p.182-3.

The Solitary Places: Elizabeth Porter

Elizabeth Porter gained her PGCE from Durham University in 1987. Since then she has taught English and Media Studies at secondary schools in the north east of England and in South Wales, and for three years with VSO she taught English in Tanzania. She has also enjoyed diverse experiences as an adult education tutor for literature, literacy and on a women's community project: English for Pregnancy. She currently teaches at a further education college. In the year 2000 she gained an MA in the teaching and practice of creative writing at Cardiff University, and she believes passionately that people of all ages can learn from creative writing, both within and outside the traditional curriculum.

I don't know what inspiration is. Perhaps it's too broad a term to be defined. Perhaps it really is the breath of the gods. But I do know what inspiration feels like, and I think and hope we all do, deep down, even if publicly we refuse to recognise that moment when we suddenly do something brilliant. It worries me that in education's current climate inspiration is tacitly dismissed as irrelevant; what matters is achievement. Many people may say it is unnecessary to justify the current obsession with achievement, for what is the point of education if not to enable learners to pass exams with better and better grades? But coexisting with this self-evident truth, we have teachers acclaimed for their excellence in facilitating achievement, and yet secretly at the end of their tether, having breakdowns, leaving the profession. Worse, we have learners who are failing on a widespread scale, and learners who are not only opting out of education, but also opting out of society itself. Our obsession with achievement has become counterproductive. The main argument of this chapter is that we need to find some way of bringing inspiration into schools, recognising its primacy and letting it survive.

Anyone who has ever *tried* to be inspired will know what an absurd enterprise such an act of will and yearning can be. Equally, anyone who has ever put their heart and soul into anything (perhaps performing a piece of music or directing a play or scoring a goal or pursuing a line of scientific enquiry or helping someone to come to terms with something very difficult) will know what it feels like to concentrate very, very hard, to make a real effort, and then suddenly to be lifted, so you find yourself momentarily somewhere higher. Maybe you had no idea how this happened; maybe afterwards you weren't even sure it *had* happened, you couldn't trust that it had happened. Maybe it took someone else to marvel or to be thankful for you to realise that you had been inspired to brilliance. I want to suggest that there are ways, not of chasing inspiration, trying to be inspired, but of showing that you recognise the possibility of inspiration, and that you would like it to be present.

Other contributors to this book have written about I-Thou encounters, the understanding that teaching is an unfinished draft and that we need, more than ever, the spaciousness of uncertainty. All of these are ways of showing this recognition, because they all have their bedrock in Possibility. But I also think that Necessity, which sometimes finds shape in what we find most appalling in schools, has its relationship with inspiration, paradoxical though that may seem. For some time now an extremely grand statement by Balzac has been repeating itself like a provocative mantra somewhere at the back of my mind: "All great passions are preceded by aversions ..." and although we may instinctively wish to resist the intriguing but perhaps also frightening notion that by going through bad experiences we will arrive somewhere altogether more exhilarating, maybe instead we should dare to go along with Balzac, and entertain the idea that there is a more vital relationship between Necessity and inspiration than our logical minds would have us believe. Perhaps our experience of what we find appalling enables us to achieve that clear, bright vision of how much better things could be. Perhaps the grind of Necessity in our schools and universities can sometimes, paradoxically, provide the conditions we need to create art.

Maybe one reason why this phrase of Balzac's has been so much in my mind is because it seems to give a shape to my own experiences of the past few years, which I want to write about briefly. I see now that I had developed an aversion to teaching; to what I felt unwillingly part of, and to the state of mind that 'being a teacher at the end of the 20th century' seemed to induce. The most frightening part of this aversion was what appeared at the time to be its irrationality, since I was teaching in a 'good' school, within a department full of people who were kind, committed, ingenious. But there were too many people with whom I wanted to have I-Thou encounters, and yet couldn't. Everyone wanted the teaching to be, far from an unfinished draft, as polished and perfect as possible, but there was simply no space in which to create this perfect ideal, and the lack of space began to make me feel frantic. In the months leading up to an Ofsted inspection, I frequently found myself in what at the time felt like a very peculiar state. Every evening when I arrived home from the school I would take a book of poems at random from a shelf, because all I wanted was to enter the separate space to be found within the poetry and stay there until my thoughts had unravelled, reconfigured, gained some support from the elegant structures created by minds other than my own. I realise now I was looking not so much for the structures themselves, as for the spaces which were integral to them, and perhaps fundamental to all works of art. I wanted space, perhaps, for still more urgent reasons than the obvious one that in teaching there is never enough time to do anything properly, let alone stop and think.

An aversion is a turning away; eventually of course I left that school – and left teaching. Within a year, however, I found myself teaching again, thanks to a greater awareness of Possibility and inspiration which in part stemmed from my involvement in the writing of this book. I feel very relieved to be free from that sense of dread and hopelessness which overwhelmed me at times, as, I suspect, it overwhelms millions of others. So, to consider what it is that is truly inspirational within teaching and learning, what it is that might enable someone to move from aversion towards something more exhilarating, or noble, or free, I want to write about some of the people I have come across in the course of being a teacher and a learner myself.

Let's go back to a squalid little shed in North Oxford; not the oak-panelled room I had anticipated but, in its own filthy way, just as impressive to me at the age of nineteen. I have finished reading my essay on Dickens (a long, dutiful essay) to the back of my tutor's head. So much for the first rule of good teaching: *make eye contact with your pupils*. At the end of the essay she half turns, a pained look on her face, and there is silence. Then, slowly, she shakes her head. "No," she says. "No. No, no, no. No. NO!" And I am devastated, but it doesn't matter, because this is a bona fide I-Thou encounter. Despite my hurt feelings I desperately want to know what there is in Dickens that she can see and that she wants me to see too – not to gratify her own ego, not to get good exam results and score in the university league tables, but because she loves literature with a passion fiercer than I have ever seen in anyone else, and partly I'm appalled by that passion, because there are more important things in life than books and plays and poems, but partly I'm intrigued by it. Eventually, after a year of bewilderment, frustration and hard work, the light shines and I too can revel in the glory of Dickens.

Jump forward several years, and I'm a new enough member of staff at the 'good' school to be pretty ecstatic and amazed at these nice children who say hello to you in the corridor, stop talking when asked, and fill their exercise books with imaginative and beautifully illustrated work. Except Joseph. Tiny for his eleven years, Joseph never smiles, and unlike other children in that blissful pre-adolescent stage, he is cynical as well as bored and disruptive. In English lessons Joseph does next to nothing (frightening admission: sometimes pupils can spend whole terms, whole academic years, *doing nothing*). Although I try to encourage him, his writing never amounts to more than a couple of misspelled, barely punctuated lines and one day, during a poetry lesson when the rest of the children are all being sweet and responsive and creative, and Joseph is being as bolshy as he can, I lose my temper. I order him to move away from the other children and sit on his own like a pariah at my desk, yelling at him something along the lines of, "Sit there, don't move, don't even look round until you've WRITTEN A POEM!!" Hardly conducive to the creative process, one would think, and Joseph slumps over the desk, head lolling on his arm, scowling at the grubby page. I leave him to it. At the end of the exhausting afternoon, when I return to see what he has done, I am amazed and humbled by the poem he has written. By any standards the poem has something to it, but coming from Joseph, and in these circumstances, it is astonishing. Of course I praise him. "Huh," he grunts. When it is eventually published in the school magazine, my colleagues remark how good the poem is, and how extraordinary that Joseph, of all people, should be the writer. Joseph confronts me, screws his face into a hideous scrunch and mutters: "You put my poem in the magazine."

"Yes," I reply, "because it was so good."

"Huh! Embarrassing!" he grunts again. But his grandmother reports that at home he's never stopped talking about his appearance in print. Here is Joseph's poem:

> I would like to paint the sound of Death
> and the sound of the Devil, burning away
> I would like to touch the reflection of wind
> on a cold day in winter
> I would like to keep the sound of gold burning red hot
> I would like to take the roar of the lion
> and keep it locked in a dark cave
> and also I would like to paint the sun's heat
> I would like to take the coldness out of ice
> and the heat out of lava
> and put the heat into ice
> and the coldness into lava
> I would like to paint the smell of wine
> and the taste
> I would like to paint the freshness
> of a giant waterfall

The poem changed something between Joseph and me. He never misbehaved for me again; instead he worked well. Later I learned of the traumatic event in Joseph's past which went some way to explaining his habitual bad behaviour, and I was shaken and very sad for him. I hope, however, he and I had just enough of an encounter, despite its totally inauspicious beginnings, to make a small difference in his life.

Another episode at that school happened some years later, but reminded me instantly of my experience with Joseph. Like him, Clare was eleven and tiny for her age, but there the similarities ended. Whereas he was surly, she was sunny, keen and 'good at English'. Many of the children in Clare's class wrote for pleasure, so I wasn't too surprised when, towards the end of the school year, she came up to me during a lesson and asked if I'd like to read a poem she'd written. Of course I said yes.

The Attacker
First he waits, waits for me.
Then he attacks.
I reach in my pocket for my weapon, but before I can use it
He attacks and I fall gasping for breath.
He's crowding me.
He's so heavy on my chest.
I'm choking, he's strangling me, I need air,
I feel sharp, stabbing pains in my chest.
I manage to pull out my weapon and use it,
In two short, sharp breaths he's gone.

But I know he will come back.

What immediately struck me was the evocation of fear and tension, the superb, spot-on, inspired positioning of the last line, even before I realised the poem was about her experience of the modern child's scourge: asthma. We talked about the poem for a while. I told her why I thought it was very good, and asked if I could read it out to the class. Now came the surprise: ".Oh, no thank you," she said politely. "I'd rather you didn't." I always tried to encourage the sharing of creative work in the classroom and normally Clare, like other children, loved hearing her work read aloud and praised – but on this occasion she didn't want public acclaim, so I respected her wishes. I learned from Clare a significant lesson about the purpose of writing, perhaps the purpose of art itself: how it isn't necessarily to do with wanting to reach a wider audience. I honestly don't think she was eager to receive even my good opinion, either; I think she showed me the poem because she knew I was interested in what writing can do, and she was aware (perhaps more than aware) that she herself had been inspired, and wanted to share the fruits of her inspiration with someone in a spirit of sheer generosity. And how similar, in a way, to Joseph: his changed behaviour growing from our shared recognition of a moment of inspiration on his part which was all the more remarkable for my best efforts to scupper it. Clare also taught me a valuable lesson about the relationship between writing and learning, as she exemplified the vital integrity pinpointed by Robert Graham when he writes of:

> ...that ancient and eternal struggle at the very heart of learning, at the very heart of growing up indeed; am I learning in order to provide myself and others with indicators of my learnedness ... or am I learning in order to stake out claims in new territory and bring these into harmonious relationship with the rest of my stakes in and true connections with the world? Am I learning for show or for real?[1]

'Learning for real' was in evidence during the year I spent working as 'Adult literacy tutor' in a hospital for adults with learning difficulties. It was a lovely job; I have never enjoyed such popularity. Whenever I turned up on a ward to collect one of the residents for their literacy session, the resident would be overjoyed to be leaving the ward, and the nurses would be overjoyed to have one less person to look after for an hour. Sadly my popularity was an indicator of how grim life generally was for everyone in that hospital, which was due to be closed down, and all the residents to be moved out to live in shared houses in the community. There were people, residents *and* staff, who had spent almost all their lives in the hospital, and they had deeply mixed feelings about leaving it. For me, one of the most striking features of the place was the schismatic ideology embodied by those who ran it: the official line was that the residents should participate in a process known rather disturbingly as 'normalisation', sometimes known less disturbingly but more perplexingly as 'social role valorisation', the gist of which was that residents should be actively encouraged to live as 'normally' as possible, regardless of their personal inclinations. In practical terms, normalisation meant living in small houses with four or five people, rather than a huge hospital with a couple of hundred. Fair enough, but it also meant that it was unacceptable for people to do things that patently weren't 'normal', e.g. for a woman called Janice to burst into coloratura arias at well-chosen inappropriate moments, such as underneath the open window of the hospital board room when various psychiatrists and executives in suits were trying to hold a sensible meeting. Those of us who enjoyed Janice's impromptu performances were scolded by management and exhorted to remember and promote the philosophy of social role valorisation. I could see their point of view but it is, I think, significant that individuality no matter how 'abnormal' was championed by the lowlier hospital staff, and 'normalisation' by the higher status, better paid experts who, like the managers and experts in our education system, have a vested interest in keeping everything very much under control.

An incident with Belinda demonstrated how my own role placed me uncomfortably between these two positions, and how 'learning for real' is the most important kind of learning. Belinda was a redoubtable figure, stumping round the hospital grounds fag in mouth whenever she was angry, which was often, and sometimes just wandering aimlessly and alone for hours and hours. The highlights of her week were her sessions with me and the dietician, because we had time to give her the attention she yearned for – it's worth saying, the attention from another human being that most of us take for granted. Belinda was in her thirties and had already been moved out of the hospital once, as part of the 'rolling resettlement programme', but the house-share hadn't worked, had been a disaster, so here she was, back in the institution. On looking through her file of notes, which covered the many years of her time in the hospital, I was horrified to read epithets such as 'manipulative' and 'selfish' applied to someone who had no chance of ever being able to read those notes for herself.

This particular morning Belinda was trying, for the umpteenth time, to write her own name, when a knock at the door heralded the arrival of Alison, Belinda's very nice occupational therapist. Nice or not, interruptions to our session were always unwelcome; Belinda gave her a sharp look. Alison apologised for interrupting and asked her to go back to her ward when we'd finished as the charge nurse wanted to arrange some money for a trip to town. An innocuous enough message, although can you imagine how horrible it must be to be in your thirties and know that other people have to administer your money for you and dole it out to you in measures which they deem appropriate? Maybe that accounts for what happened next, or maybe not. Belinda shouted, "NO!" There was an awful pause. Alison and I looked at each other tentatively. Belinda quivered. "It won't take five minutes, Belinda," Alison said, but "No!" Belinda forced out the word between clenched teeth as she drummed frantically on the table with her fists. "No, no, no!" she shouted, and then she spat, "Get out!"

Quite rightly Alison took exception to this and said so, but Belinda was in a rage. "We'll just have to sort this out later," Alison said, and left.

I don't mind admitting that I was scared. The adult literacy tutor's room was extremely small and secluded; Belinda was large and very, very angry, angrier than I had ever seen her. While I was rapidly running through the possibilities: whether to say, "Never mind," or simply continue with the session as if nothing had happened, Belinda carried on quivering, but this time in a different way, and her lip began to wobble. I was amazed by what she said next.

"Oh," she said. "Oh, poor old Alison. I shouldn't have done that, should I?" All her anger had vanished, leaving nothing but remorse and pity, and a humility that would not go amiss in people far more privileged than she, far more capable of making massive errors of judgement with dreadful consequences. I stopped being scared, and felt humbled instead. When I told Alison later on what Belinda had said, she too was amazed and touched. It was a pretty unusual incident, not least because one of the plights of the people who lived in that institution was that they had so little control over their lives, they rarely had the opportunity to be generous in any way, perhaps least of all to show the kind of emotional generosity which entails putting yourself in someone else's place even when you yourself are feeling powerless and frustrated. It was another example of a kind of I-Thou encounter taking place against all the odds, and as with my pupil Joseph I was hard-pressed to explain how Belinda's response came about. Do we *need* to know why Belinda was able to create that encounter? Or should we concentrate our energies on being able to recognise inspiration when we see it, and maybe living in hope that if such moments of inspiration can happen once, they can happen again? We live in an age in which schools are constantly required to analyse, explain, account for their achievements or lack of achievements, but learners such as Belinda and Joseph seem to be inspired in spite of, rather than because of, the system they are forced to endure.

I want to write next about Dickens's depiction of a society that is sick to the heart, because it seems to me that he gives us a timely warning about what we are doing to each other and to ourselves, and yet simultaneously he is enabling us to see that there is another way of doing things. *Hard Times* famously begins with a school in which imagination is forbidden and only facts are considered to be of any educational value. It is interesting that Dickens makes Louisa Gradgrind his main character, even though she is not a pupil at this school but the daughter of its owner, Mr. Gradgrind. Perhaps Dickens was acutely aware that those such as Gradgrind who have the power to inflict damage on our society are also and inevitably inflicting damage on themselves and those whom they love. Louisa and her brother Tom grow up emotionally stunted because without imagination there can be no feeling - thus, Tom grows up to care only about pleasing himself, through money and alcohol. This repression of feeling is highly dangerous; Louisa is human so she must love and care for someone, but the person she loves is her brother, and she proves it by marrying, at Tom's mercenary request, his boss Bounderby, a hypocrite who is old enough to be her father. But Dickens presents Louisa as so enigmatic, so unable to say what she feels, that it is very hard on a first reading of the novel to take in exactly what she is doing and why. Some years ago I taught this novel to a GCSE class, and one of my pupils, a very quiet girl, summed up Louisa with a phrase which left me and the rest of the class stunned by its brilliance and sheer engagement: "She is the locked diary that everyone wants to read." Yes, we all said, that's it. And by the end of the novel it is as if we *are* reading the diary and it does not make sense. Dickens does not reward Louisa later on in the novel for running away from the young man who tries to seduce her into adultery. He does not reward her for running to her benighted father Gradgrind and confronting him with the malformed fruits of his educational experiment. Louisa's honour is preserved, but she never makes a happy marriage and is merely contented at the end of the story to watch over the children of her friend Sissy the circus girl – children who grow up free to imagine whatever they please.

There comes a point, Dickens is saying, when it is too late to save people. He evokes the terrible transformation that may occur when the imagination is given no outlet very early on in *Hard Times*, when Louisa shows a yearning, not for emotion itself, but for the *knowledge* of emotion; the vicarious experience of it. Sissy the circus girl has neither father nor mother, and has been taken by Gradgrind into his own home for the sake of his experiment. Louisa observes Sissy's grief and wants to know more about her parents.

"Did your father love her?" Louisa asked these questions with a strong, wild, wandering interest peculiar to her; an interest gone astray, like a banished creature, and hiding in solitary places.

Even by Dickens' standards this is an extraordinary simile, and worth unravelling. Louisa's 'strong, wild, wandering interest' in someone else's feelings, someone else's narrative, is the imaginative impulse (or the human desire for conversation) which her father rejects. That the imagination should be at once 'banished' (suggesting that it does have a rightful home) and 'wild' seems contradictory – is Dickens saying that an imagination which is neglected, left to fend for itself, will become feral and dangerous? Dangerous, and yet, perhaps, indestructible, as it lurks in those 'solitary places'?

I find it fascinating and disturbing that *Hard Times* does not present us with a neatly polarised reading of human relationships and why they succeed or fail. Gradgrind is not the only inadequate father in the novel; Sissy's father disappears, effectively abandoning his daughter, and what saves her is not the return of the father (a scene which Dickens could so easily have written) but her own strength of mind. Dickens does, I think, show that the imaginative impulse can be allied with the moral impulse; Sissy cares for Mrs. Gradgrind when she is dying, and does a good job of bringing up the younger Gradgrinds. Louisa, whose imagination is feral, tries to do what is best for Tom and only succeeds in enabling him to become even more wicked.

But Dickens is *not* saying that a free imagination is the prerequisite of morality. How could he, of all people, have claimed that? In *The Invisible Woman*, her brilliant biography of the actress Ellen Ternan who was Dickens's mistress, Clare

Tomalin carefully and compassionately shows how Dickens invested a phenomenal amount of ingenuity in conducting a love affair that lasted many years with a girl young enough to be his daughter (as Louisa is young enough to be Bounderby's daughter), while he was married, and while he was revered as the most famous man in Britain.

The point is that people are allowed to make mistakes. When the story of the love affair became public, many years after Dickens's death, people were deeply distressed to find that the great man had feet of clay. Now, Tomalin's research contributes to our knowledge of Dickens and of Victorian society, and also, more importantly, to our understanding of why women are in the position we are in today. But Dickens's novels are still read and marvelled over, because he was inspired, and I suggest that his mistakes and lies and image-making all contributed, in some way or another, to that inspiration without which the world would be a poorer place.

Hard Times is not a novel about the damage an education system can do to society, it's a novel about the way in which a society's values, which are reflected in its education system, can damage people. At present in our society some terrible damage is being done - but let's look now at an education system in another culture, and see how real learning can happen *despite* the restrictions of the system if the society itself is fundamentally good enough.

When I was seven, I was lucky enough to have a teacher called Mrs. Scott who inspired me with an intense curiosity about other countries and cultures in her lessons about Peru and Canada and East Africa. It was largely due to her superb teaching that years later I realised what I most wanted to do was to satisfy my curiosity by living and working somewhere as different as possible, and so I went to East Africa to do voluntary work as a teacher in Tanzania. The development agency who financed my post would not be pleased to read that my primary motive was curiosity; they have a mission statement (not a bad one, as mission statements go) which would amply disguise my original motives. Sadly there is little variation on the two polarities of public statements made by westerners who have lived for any length of time in a developing country – the usual versions are: "The people are wonderful!" or the jaded "The whole country is a shambles and corruption is so rife, they'll never be able to sort it out." However, I hope that by touching on what it felt like to be in the middle of what at times felt like literally 'the spaciousness of uncertainty', I can show something of what we might learn from Tanzania's approach to education.

Ofsted inspectors remind me very much of the Experts: the Europeans who would occasionally descend on that little town in northern Tanzania to give the local population the benefit of their expertise and their general right-on sophistication. At times their arrogance beggared belief, as did their apparently total disrespect for the lives of people who, unlike them, would never travel to and fro between Europe and Africa, because they would never, even in their wildest dreams, be able to afford the fare. An image sums it all up: a huge drill, like a giant long-legged sci-fi insect, which stood on the plain at the bottom of the hill by the school, a plain which for part of every year was taken up by a seasonal lake, a breeding ground for mosquitoes which brought malaria. The water in this lake was undrinkable. European Experts *insisted* that if only you drilled deep enough you would find pure water beneath this murky lake, water which could be piped all round the town and transform people's lives. They had been saying this for years, but, well, the locals had to organise themselves, they had to be motivated to do something about their own problems. The Norwegian government funded the drilling project, the giant insect that crouched over the plain for nine long months, and at the end of that time all they found was mud and silt. There were technical explanations. The Norwegians were aghast; the Experts disappeared as suddenly as they had come, leaving only silence. The locals shrugged and picked up their buckets for the long walk to the standpipe. They had been *so certain*, those Experts with their blonde hair and their Landcruisers – dig deep enough and you will find water; work hard enough, organise yourselves efficiently, and you will solve the problems of a nation's children. But what if the real problem is a fundamental lack of respect, an inability to have a conversation in no-man's-land, where, despite our differences, maybe even *because of* our differences, we might be able to reflect on the absurdity of the world we live in, a world in which millions of deaths are thought to be a fair price for national boundaries and the economic stability of a minority?

This fertile coffee-growing area of northern Tanzania was often so dry that the red earth would become pounded and compacted into a fine, insidious dust. The students, aged between 15 and 20, cleaned the village school themselves. They cleaned it and cleaned it. Every morning at half past seven a team of students could be seen with brooms made of branches, sweeping the dust, sweeping out the foot prints and animal prints and smoothing the dust into elegant fan shapes. Ten minutes later these patterns would be trampled over and scuffed again, but every day this elaborate sweeping took place. I'm not sure why this image has remained with me, but perhaps it has something to do with tenacity, and pride in making something beautiful out of something bothersome and mundane. Dickens would probably have felt quite at home in that village school where the students were crammed three to a desk in bare classrooms and those who couldn't remember their nine times table were beaten; where lessons were frequently cancelled for water-collecting expeditions or weeding on the school farm, and the students tried to catch up at night, poring over their few books by candlelight. The school was complex and puzzling and frustrating, as all schools are. As a foreigner, I was more puzzled than most, and frequently let my frustrations get the better of me - I never got used to turning up to teach a class, only to find that they were on 'farm duty'. However, there were glimpses of real encounters, evidence that people in that school knew how to talk to each other, despite what an Ofsted inspector or an Expert would have said.

I remember one incident in particular, which encapsulates what it is that all of us who work in schools need to preserve. Several weeks into the new academic year, during morning break the teachers were sitting in the staffroom drinking tea when a visitor was ushered in by Mr Uo, the school accountant. The visitor was a young boy dressed in the garb favoured by men of the local tribe, the Iraqw: a long blanket wrapped around his body and flung over one shoulder. He carried the traditional stick across the back of his neck, like a yoke. Mr Uo, who was something of a showman, announced dramatically that the boy had been walking for days from a remote village, "In the heart of the bush!" The boy stood before Mr. Mano the headmaster, bewildered, clinging onto his stick, answering Mr. Mano's questions in barely audible Swahili. Yes, he had passed the primary school leaver's exam and now he wanted to enter Form One of our secondary school. "Have you got the fees?" asked Mr. Mano, ever the pragmatist, and a fistful of Tanzanian shilling notes was produced from within the swathes of blanket. Mr. Mano then briskly gave him the lowdown on the school – and it was very different from the PR job you'd hear in a British secondary school – telling him about uniform, dormitories, rules, duties. "Got water in your village? There's no water here, you know. Well, you'll get used to it soon enough." The rest of the staff were laughing. Then, just when I thought the 'interview' was over, Mr. Mano and the boy suddenly spoke to each other in a rapid volley of Kilraqw, the language of the local tribe, officially frowned on within the education system and for sound reasons, since one of Julius Nyerere's triumphs was to avert inter-tribal conflict by making Swahili the lingua franca of Tanzania. Kilraqw was a strange, incomprehensible language, notoriously difficult for other Tanzanians, let alone for me. I remember how exasperated I used to feel when, having slogged at my Swahili in order to be able to talk to people, they would switch to their tribal language and I wouldn't be able to understand a word. But on this occasion, listening to the head master and the boy from the remote village in the bush, speaking to each other *in their own language*, I didn't mind a bit. Even so, at the time I felt baffled and faintly disquieted. Why were the staff laughing? Were they laughing at the boy? Or, all good Iraqw men, were they laughing at themselves, what they had once been, and what they really still were, despite their teaching diplomas and their carefully saved-for second hand suits? Was there really anything so funny in the disparity between model secondary school student and boy from the bush, given the effort he'd made to get here?

With hindsight, all that mattered was that encounter between headmaster and boy, where I do not know what was said (perhaps it is in the nature of I-Thou encounters that only those directly involved can really understand), but where the literal speaking of the same language created something more significant than the words themselves. A week later that boy from the bush, very smart in his white school uniform shirt and his khaki trousers, was sitting with his mates, laughing and busily writing down verbs in his exercise book during my Form One English class.

I believe that Ofsted is missing a vital point about the language in which we speak to each other when it seeks, for example, to write an assessment of how a school creates opportunities for spiritual development in a terse paragraph or two bemoaning the lack of singing in assemblies. Do such paragraphs not seem a contradiction in terms to those who write them? I would guess there are inspectors who are anguished by such contradictions, just as there are countless teachers, myself included, who loathe themselves when writing reports on their students, never mind how dextrous we are at balancing the necessary and the possible – and who feel impotent to do anything about this necessity in the face of the bureaucracy that pays our wages and determines educational policy. Perhaps I'm too easily scared by the permanence, the officialdom of the printed word; perhaps I shouldn't be so worried about what is written down when we all know it's ridiculous and there are worse outrages being perpetrated in the name of education. However, there is one person who I can't get out of my mind at the moment, an Ofsted inspector who visited a music lesson being taught by a woman widely acknowledged to be, not only a superb musician and teacher but a kind and good person. At the start of the lesson, which she was teaching to some Year 11 boys not renowned for their musical talent, the inspector had gone through some schemes of work or other such documentation with this woman and had criticized them – in the classroom, in front of the boys. The teacher then had to teach the class and, unnerved by the public criticism, harassed, exhausted from the strain of months of pre-inspection preparations, she began to cry – but she doggedly carried on teaching while the unmusical boys looked on aghast, and the inspector continued to make notes on his clipboard. Eventually one of the boys could stand it no longer; he ran out of the room, down the corridor and burst into the classroom of the head of music. "Miss, you'd better come." When the head of music found her colleague in tears and the inspector taking notes, she invited him into the stock cupboard and tore him off a strip. Subsequently he did receive an official reprimand. The tearful music teacher recovered; the unmusical Year 11 boys recovered (although the incident must have been deeply unpleasant for them), but the person I'm most concerned about is the inspector. What was going through his mind, as he sat there with his clipboard watching her cry? What went through his mind at the end of the day, when he went home with the official reprimand still ringing sharply in his ears? 'Stupid woman'? 'It's a tough life, being an inspector'? 'Whoops, I overstepped the mark there...'? I hope he felt profoundly guilty. I hope he recognised himself stepping over that moral line that exists in a parallel universe to Ofsted. I hope he found himself in no-man's-land. Because if he didn't, there's no hope for him at all.

The Orwellian perverseness which this story illustrates make me wonder what we can all do (because we are all caught up and implicated in it) to avoid losing all feeling, becoming numb, and not just unknowable, which is fine, but *alone*, which is not. It does seem to me that the answer must lie in sometimes turning away from the system, not in a spirit of cowardice, but because in Balzac's words aversions can lead to passion. I'm saying that sometimes we have to know what it is that we can't bear, in order to find out what it is that we most love. I want now to write about François Truffaut's film, *Fahrenheit 451*.

I was seventeen when I first saw this strange, perplexing film, which many critics have dismissed as being inferior to the director's other work. It gripped me, particularly the stunning final scene which I have often watched again in my imagination over the years, trying to recall the words, the music, the feeling the film had given me. Truffaut makes us ask *why* we read, and what literature means, by presenting us with a dystopia where imagination is vilified as an enemy of the state; where proto-Nazi 'firemen' set fire to and destroy books because books are dangerous and make people unhappy. We see the passage of one fireman, Montag, from stultifying conformity to a freedom that is dangerous, yet makes him come alive. Every evening after his destructive day's work Montag travels home on a commuter train packed with dull-eyed commuters to his box-like house where his wife Linda has spent all day popping pills and watching 'The Family', a pathetic (and yet also sinisterly prescient) travesty of interactive TV. One evening Montag is approached on the train by a girl called Clarice. Why she chooses him is never made clear; perhaps she sees in him a potential sensitivity or a sadness, or perhaps she acts out of extraordinary courage, since she asks Montag whether he ever reads the books he burns. "Why should I?" Montag replies. "First, I'm not interested, second, I've got better things to do and third, it is forbidden." But Montag is about to change irrevocably; Clarice has inspired him (another I-Thou encounter), and the book he subsequently steals, takes home, hides and reads while his wife sleeps, is that most elusive of fictions: *David Copperfield*. It begins:

> Whether I shall turn out to be the hero of my own life, or whether that station shall be held by anyone else, these pages must show ...

And on reading that first, gloriously uncertain page, Montag's life is transformed. In one of the most disturbing scenes of the film he arrives home one day to find his wife entertaining three of her vapid friends. Irritated to the limit by their complacency, driven to make them *feel* something, Montag brings out the illegal book and forces them to listen as he reads aloud the chapter in which David realises that his young wife Dora is dying. The women are outraged by Montag's 'crime', but one of them begins to weep at the story. What prompts her tears? Not empathy, much less catharsis; these are the tears of someone who, maybe for the first time ever, is acknowledging that the world is not a safe and happy place.

After this, the events of the film escalate. The firemen raid Clarice's house, and her aunt chooses to be burned along with her books. We see the chic sixties paperbacks with their broad bands of colour blacken and shrivel to ashes, "like flower petals or butterflies," as Montag's chief fondly observes, rather in the manner of an Ofsted inspector complimenting some aspect of a school before failing it.

Montag's wife leaves him and betrays him. He escapes to join the community of the Book People, who live in a birch forest on the shores of a lake. There he meets Clarice again; Clarice who is also *The Memoirs of Saint-Simon*, and he meets *Pride and Prejudice*, Sartre's *The Jewish Question, Alice in Wonderland, Waiting for Godot*, and many others, for the task of the Book People is to memorise and thus *become* their favourite books. By reciting the books to each other and to their children, they ensure that they will survive the holocaust. In the film's beautiful closing frames, we see the Book People, some of them in pairs, some alone, walking through the birch forest as the snow is falling, and we hear the murmur of many voices momentarily separating into the fragile, crystalline, unique structures of our language.

The film, representing the necessary dangers of our inner world and the way in which our identities are so inextricably linked with what we write and what we read, also provides a paradigm of what teaching can be: entering into community, bravely crossing all the boundaries which separate teaching and reading, learning and writing. Yet the film begins with aversion: that hatred of books which stems from a state-induced hatred of individuality. The triumphant irony is that aversion turns out to be merely one stage on the way to passion. However, it must be remembered that the film does present a dystopia, a society in which things have gone much too far in the wrong direction, and as in the bleak conclusion of *Hard Times*, Montag's freedom is won at a terrible price. He becomes a murderer, turning the flame gun on another fireman. When I was seventeen and saw the film for the first time I didn't realise that Clarice and Linda were both played by Julie Christie. Perhaps Truffaut's decision to cast her in both roles tells us something about his perception of a society in which imagination, inspiration and Possibility are vilified, but in which the individual still has the chance to save himself or herself. Clarice's brave, life-changing conversation with Montag takes place within the spaciousness of uncertainty, and this leads me to suggest that one resource which we all have in coping with our current Hard Times is our essential ability to participate in the conversation that sometimes takes the form of a work of art: an ability that we ought to be fostering like mad, not only in our schools but also in all our other educational institutions. University departments which get slammed for encouraging their undergraduates to do creative writing are as much at the sharp end of the debate as schools which dare to assert that it's OK for their pupils to make the occasional spelling mistake!

Maybe one reason why we're loath to encourage such conversations is that we're aware of the threat they pose to who we think we are. The art critic Peter Fuller has described the 'elusive negative emotion' he felt when looking at a painting and eloquently traces this emotion (which we might call an aversion) to a fundamental stage in the process of forming identity; of discovering who we are:

> The unease or anxiety, I am now convinced, relates to that earliest fear of the infant of an interruption in what Winnicott called 'going on being', the threat of annihilation of the ego.[2]

This explanation for the psychological basis of aversion to art also accounts for the sense of danger experienced when crossing the boundaries between teaching and learning. The threat of annihilation of the ego must surely be what we dread as we send ourselves into the spaciousness of uncertainty, offering up what we have created, what we have *done*, into an encounter with another, who could be teacher, reader, student, inspector. When we give ourselves to such encounters, we risk rejection. And in order to cope, what we need to do is what all creative artists need to do: understand that the work is not the same as the self, and that as long as we are met by *somebody*, as long as the conversation takes place at some time, we will not be annihilated.

Fuller also explains that what D.W. Winnicott has termed the 'potential space ... the third area of human living, one neither inside the individual nor outside in the world of shared reality' is essential long beyond infancy: it is a space where creativity can happen:

> The capacity to explore and investigate this 'potential space' in a situation of trust, allows the individual to develop his internal sense of space and integration, his sense of external reality, and his ability to act imaginatively and creatively upon the latter.[3]

Perhaps this 'potential space' is to be found when we cross over the boundaries of our roles as teacher, learner, reader, writer, inspector. In the act of crossing over to take part in a conversation, the whole concept of 'boundary' ceases to have metaphorical connotations of the one-dimensional line, evoking crude distinctions between all the different roles which Necessity requires us to play, and becomes instead something which is far from one-dimensional: a space where, 'in a situation of trust', real learning takes place. But crossing the boundaries is not easy. Dickens knew this when he left Louisa Gradgrind's imagination hiding in its solitary places; Truffaut knew this when he left the Book People hiding in the birch forest where the snow falls.

People take each other by surprise all the time. The same variations on love, rejection, betrayal are played out endlessly, and yet we're still surprised by what we can do to and for each other. It seems to me that this surprise is perhaps related to our fear of Possibility: the fear which might lead us to say to a student, "I don't think you're university material', or of a class, "they're hopeless", because these statements seem to be stronger than saying, "I don't know." Ability is a relative concept; learners surprise their teachers all the time, and yet how many of us ever learn *not* to be surprised? Agnosticism feels like a big, dark space, a no-man's-land between teacher and student, or perhaps an unknown forest that you wander through, unable to be sure when you'll come out into the light again. We can't crawl through such spaces with a measuring tape and a clipboard, pretending we know how to describe this place, pretending we know once and for all whether what's happening here is good and enduring or false and a waste of time.

What I'm suggesting is that we need a bit of time in schools for entering that space. The time needs to be sacrosanct. And I think at the moment it's very, very hard for any of us to make time, in an educational climate where anything, even spiritual development, is up for assessment. So my plea is for Ofsted to back off, to leave spiritual development well alone. Concurrently, schools need to be brave about taking risks which should include letting brilliance go unsung –

unsung, rather than unnoticed – and which would enable us at last to recognise, appreciate and learn from the inspired flashes of brilliance for which the special needs pupils, the Josephs and the Belindas, have as much capacity as the all-A student. If we persist in celebrating only the top grades, in valuing 'intelligence' and 'achievement' and making these the measurable summits of our system, how can we claim to be a compassionate society? How can we be alert to the Possibility that is the key to co-existing with Necessity, if we cannot let ourselves share each other's work in progress, our poor rough drafts, and acknowledge that these are just as precious as the final, polished piece?

Notes

(1) Robert Graham, 'Taking Each Other Seriously' in *Priorities in Education* (Durham: Fieldhouse, 1996), pp. 42-43.

(2) Peter Fuller, *Art and Psychoanalysis* (London: Writers and Readers Publishing Cooperative Ltd., 1980), p.202.

(3) Ibid.

A Forest: Graham Tyrer

*Graham was a student of Bob Graham's in 1981-2.
He taught in Shropshire, Norfolk and now Warwickshire where
he is currently Headteacher of Ash Green School. Graham gives
regular national training in literacy across the curriculum for the
National Literacy Trust, the Specialist Schools and Academies Trust
and the National Breakthrough Project. He developed the Learning to
Lead programme for the Warwickshire LA and led Warwickshire's first
NCSL Networked Learning Community, the Warwickshire Inclusion
Network. Graham acts and directs in Stratford upon Avon's local theatres.
He describes himself as a "permanent optimist" about the
future of education. Of his time at Durham, Graham says:
"Being taught by Bob Graham was the richest
learning experience of my life."*

*The question is, shall it or shall it not be linear history? I've always thought a
kaleidoscopic view might be an interesting heresy. Shake the tube and see what
comes out. Chronology irritates me. There is no chronology inside my head.*

Penelope Lively: Moon Tiger

What have I written? It's how it seems when I really think about it. There are many
times and people and places here. I wanted to see what would happen if I mixed
them all up, what might happen if I introduced one thing to another, nervously
positioning times, people and places next to each other. It's accidental collisions
I wanted to create, the stumbling into something new. Having a humility that a
more conventional structure might deny. You know, like when a lesson shatters
in the perfection of its timing, when each second marches in time with the next
but they've never really gone anywhere. Somehow the more security you expect,
the less happens. Being open to surprise, event, word, makes possible a depth
of experience stifled by regimented time.

Too much time and too many perfectly decent words are locked away in
frameworks and over prescriptive strategies. I've written them myself, still do as
a bulwark against the noise and clutter of too many thoughts, ideas, and people.
This project has been an opportunity to walk outside the defence lines and see
what else is there.

Some of the best lessons have said the most in silences and doubts and drafts.

I carry these memories round all the time, every day. Writing them has meant giving a little time to sifting through some of the thoughts, shades and brilliant, brilliant lights of what seems to have happened.

It covers times when I've been pupil, trainee and then English teacher, Head of English, Senior Teacher and Deputy Head. Mixed comprehensives in Shropshire, Norfolk, Durham and Warwickshire. There are also, oddly, occasional references to times spent acting with local theatre groups, experiences that have helped me see things differently. It's that stage and classroom thing: so many similarities, terrors and excitements, truths and masks.

The bits in italic are just a forest. I wrote them and I can't remember when. But it seems important and I don't know why.

Where the little stream runs it cuts deeply but without any fuss and without anyone noticing. It's well gone now, the path, can't see it when you turn round. Underfoot the ground is slippery with pine needles and bunches of smooth tree root.

He tells me, "We say we believe in poetry. So we should allow ourselves to live it." I walk into my friend's class where he teaches with a passion and energy and an open heart, searching with the children for just the right word, just the right phrase to shape, let loose, clarify, mystify an imagined moment. A forest is all they are describing. I see them begin to live there, in the classroom, I see it shift and change on the whiteboard as words are swapped, altered, crossed out, underlined, added to. The sensation of forest grows more prickly, more smelly, and wet and thick. In the eyes of the children is a delicate uncertainty, a wondering, questioning loss of self. They are just at the point where there is a meeting between self and other, where the forest is beginning to grow around them and it could be a little bit frightening and a little bit risky and scary and it might be safer to stay where you are with the smooth formica desk and clattering pencil tin lid. They are just on that border between places of surefooted, labeled security and a country without maps where new emotions are born every minute and new sights to envelop, transport, changes are brought into relief by the dream of the word. I see them wondering just how far they can imagine, whether it's all right to be as bold as this, to dwell in this world where words can seem bluntly safe in solid strokes of ink and then suddenly leap into dusty parts of you, inhabiting with transient but lasting brilliance what had been silently, happily backwatered.

My friend is a poet. The teaching is a draft, unfinished business. He has no plan in front of him, just the happy accident of intuition and a tolerant open sensibility. He has a sense of what ought to be happening in the drama of the room and a risk taking essential delight about what might be said, thought, felt, or imagined. I feel the risk, the thrill of not knowing what may appear.

I think to myself: this is the sort of journey I want to take, with someone who has a map but not a route march, someone who leads an exploration rather than conquers with cold, deliberate certainty.

Later, I feel it myself, when we talk together, my Year 10 and I about what is happening on the front cover of a series of supernatural fictions and then on the opening pages of the same novels. I feel a sense of real voice, children feeling the strength of their own voices, trying to describe the effect the images have by using poetic language: 'It's like a dream I have of snakes, all around me," "It's like a kite, being floating, sort of, it's got a sharpness and it floats and you don't know where the wind will take it."

There are two children in this school who I cannot bring any further together than two completely different countries. One hides behind books and believes he cannot be seen because he cannot see me. The other uses the book as a door into her own worlds of dark and brilliant imaginative oceans. Mark grins at me amiably and forces his pen across the page. Helen cannot stop her pen until she encounters her own anxiety and agony, one of choice, which word, which metaphor, which texture, mood, atmosphere, how to achieve the birth of emotion in blottable ink.

One day, Mark tries to escape from the classroom: he ducks down behind the book and edges his desk nearer and nearer the fire escape. Part of me wonders how far he will get and whether he will take the whole desk with him in his bid for freedom.

We are told to shut our eyes because new curtains have been ordered for the school hall which we must not look at. We are in a land of bitter magic. Our sight will destroy the curtains so we must keep our hands over our shut eyes to make double sure. We will be punished if we look, if we even peep. During the set change for the play our heads bow, our eyes shut, our hands fasten over our eyes. But I cannot resist it, my fingers ever so slightly part, my head lifts just a fraction, just a tiny bit. There are no curtains. The headteacher stands guard as furniture is moved around on stage.

When it's over we hear, as we hear at the end of every assembly: 'Stand up Mr Jones' class and lead out quietly.' We do and walk to the back of the hall, down the glassy clean corridor out of the school and onto the path up which my brother ran into the playground on his first day, coat flapping wildly like a bird ready for flight. His face was bright with joy.

The street is oddly quiet. Being out of school on a school day has a delicious, illicit excitement even though our teacher is leading us to the Temperance Hall where our classroom is. We pass the sweet shop with its soft wooden floorboards and heavy piles of sherbet and lucky bags and lemony lollipops. It is always dark in there and the woman who owns it doesn't seem to fit, she is so fierce.

We are like a parade, something a bit special, such a straight line going to a special place.

When the wind is really rough, it seems to want to get in and join us. It tears at the roof, hauling down the sheets of corrugated iron. We just carry on. I sit next to a huge oil burner which is caged in as if it has been naughty or needs to be held back in case it escapes and runs amok.

The loo outside doesn't even have a roof which means boys can and do climb up the walls from the outside and laugh at you when you take a pee.

I don't think I say much and I have a friend who is German and cannot say much either. I have another friend who is Canadian who speaks all the time and tells me I know things when I don't: "Go on, you know that, you know that."

In the corner of another room there are huge red sails. They say *Happy Christmas* in Chinese. I am called up to the teacher. When I cannot see what is wrong in my work, she hits me on the back of my legs but I still can't see it. She hits me again and again and even though I'm crying I still can't see it. The sails are as still as anything, three of them, with golden writing on the soft, soft silk.

Water dances and slides over the rocks. It's difficult to know where to cross.

Hannah always has something to say, whatever question I ask, she puts up her hand and says something. Many times she starts to get an idea together and it just collapses in the air around her. I try to reassure her by saying: "Don't worry, it's good to think aloud." I hope this makes a difference.

I believe I can hear her thoughts like: how can it matter what I think? I have never really thought anything worthwhile. I believe I can see cliff faces of words being stared up at in dismay; some of them are so angular and sharp and seem to offer so few footholds.

But when they write I can feel their trust. They slip and slide on the ascent but we are roped together.

James reads the poem and writes: *It is as if the wind is an animal they don't know anything about, can't control. It's going to devour them. Even the skyline wants to get away.*

Her face was so full of tired pain. The desk itself kept her and us at bay. What secrets she must have held behind those eyes. What sadness in the raise of her hand, in the sweep of its cut through the air. Her gift. Her prison.

In the dark of the theatre where I teach this A level class, the students read poetry to one another. They want it dark to give things an edge. There is something there in their bright faces even before they put on masks. They dizzy themselves with spinning words and I sit, the only one unmasked, taking care of them, hoping with them, helping them out of and into themselves. I am as scared as they were when they began. But now they breathe confidence in steady rhythms, sitting in this well of the stage. And from far away places, new phrases and words have arrived taking their place with us, hastily scribbled on nearby paper, without planning or expectation, on and on they write and read and invent and feel astonished by what faces them when they stop and I calm them and take off their masks and invite them to read.

When it is over, silence settles on the space like a huge, invisible bird.

He gets up, darts over to the metal lockers and begins head butting them really hard. I stop him and he lashes, whirlwinds his arms around, face knotted in anguish. I feel like crying and screaming. On his desk, lie several crumpled fists of paper, the abandoned beginnings of a story about a spooky old house. He brings up massive, hammering sobs, shocking the classroom assistant and me even though we have seen it before. Most of the class have lived with this for years and take no notice, calling out for coloured pencils or for help with spellings or more paper or because they cannot get started or for rescue from the wasp which has begun a leisurely sweep of the room cutting its way neatly through the threads of my lessons.

I manage to steer Michael to the door and into the corridor to calm him down. He kicks the radiator and then a chair, but he has stopped shouting.

In my room I find two girls sitting at the back, softly whispering to each other. I say: "You can't be in here, I'm afraid. It's break. You'll have to go outside." There's no response except the girls look at me and then turn away. "Come on. Get some fresh air. It's good for you."
One of them speaks up: "We don't like break. Can't we stay here?"
"No, sorry." They don't argue and head for the door. I see them turn the wrong way down the corridor. I call after them: "The playground's down there.

Where are you going?"

"To hide," says one of them. "Just to hide."

The river is like the child of the mountain. I struggle to share my sense that some door has opened with these words. Sarah senses it too. Melissa writes: *No one notices me, they kick me as they go by. At night I dream of a new coat of paint.* Her poem gives a voice to what? The skirting board of course! Windows and doors open by fragments and then are suddenly thrown wide, almost off their hinges. I try to share the storm of words with everyone else in the class; I show them how conventions can intensify the energy. I cloze a poem, they guess at the possibilities which are better, richer than the original. I ask them to talk about the effects of their choices. I try to make presents out of the metalanguage and it works, just works. After all, the objective and the subjective must both live alongside one another, the glorious moment and the reflection.

A colleague has taught his students that the weapon of strike action is a valuable aid against the oppressor. Now his students have written to me saying they will strike unless they get a room change. I discuss this with the teacher, telling him his teaching focus has been inappropriate. He is appalled and asks me whether I was on the side of Margaret Thatcher during the miners' strike. Only what I consider is his desperation prevents me from feeling deep anger at his question. I insist English teaching isn't about strike action. "What is it about?" my colleague asks.

I am in the wings, breathless with poised tense horror. Then, suddenly out there, the darkness of faces, endless above and around and below. And inside, words start forming, without my control, without permission.

It is a strange land, here at the front of the class. Dreams, half formed words and nightmares lurk inside piles of shabby books, in corners, floating amid the golden dust of the late afternoon light. From somewhere comes the courage to write, the audacity to make a mark, to write something. *He hears footsteps crunching the autumnal leaves.*

Images never seem to emerge into perfect clarity, there are always shadows in the edge, there are always blurs of colour and feeling in the garden, the street, and the moment.

When I raise my head at last and look out at the endless rows of seats, the exposure is almost too much to bear, the embrace of fear too tight to resist, too seductive to revile. And I hear words, carving their way through the air, through the light.

There will be a bell and a change and another lesson to go to, Chemistry or RE or something. But here, where fragments of story lie bundled in some oddly tidy order, where the ink is dark light, here is my island, my safety.

Someone reaches behind them to close the window but when it shuts, it seems to turn the air in the room to a solid block, still and weighty. Eyes cloud. Words turn cold. The agenda in front of us is, though, full of potential: the phrase *raising achievement* could mean anything, if we wanted. But it lies, wounded, on the paper. No one wants to tend it. Their own territories are too full of anxiety. Fences appear round each Head of Department and the sniping, mostly defensive, begins.

"We won't do anything," says someone, *"it's all a waste of time."* But I think: your fences are too high for words to climb them.

I stand at the board asking for discussion. We talk about what we shall study this term. I list possible options and the students talk about additions they would like to see. Then we vote on what the priorities are. There's a sense in which words feel they belong here, they make things deeper, richer. Sian asks whether she can study something which didn't get voted on, and yes, I can let her. It'll take a lot of support, but that's what I'm here for. She says: *"I really feel heard here."*

There is a sense of too many eyes and of vertigo. Knowing you must say something. Dampness making her huddle inside six feet of fur. A blue nose, literally blue with the cold. Her voice makes each moment brittle and sharp edged. We are so good at disguise. When you are called to the front and given the chalk, it is an award for simply not knowing and suddenly all languages become foreign and you do not know how to say anything.

And suddenly they are all over the room, bits of paper I've hidden. Murdstone is somewhere shredded into brutal sentences, three times larger than the print from the Christmas present book I have used, its spine torn down one side and no inscription – never asked for one, never even thought about it at the time.

'He should be looked after. We will look after him.' His day planner, green desiccated cover. 'We know what to do. We should have a meeting with his parents.'

I cannot move. I feel questions crowd for attention but dare not choose any of them.

Wasn't like this just now, in the circle, I spoke and spoke and spoke. Later watching the video I will regret that, knowing this even then, even at the time. Paper flutters, folded, refolded. Sitting on at least three chairs which balance, just: he makes them teeter, knows the sound they will make if they fall. I finish the syllable. He climbs over it and drops down the other side doesn't look at me, don't think he knows ·I'm there. Plotting voices. Copperfield, Copperfield, shouldn't be left alone, shouldn't be treated like this. If only there was some safety. 'But there isn't much, anyway perhaps he asked for it. Perhaps he needed a good battering. Like you.' Sitting at my desk, stray pens and papers.

Knowing you must say something. Glass on both sides and a neat noticeboard, posters of food and gleaming bottles and slices of Normandy. So far away, so long down the middle of the room, a box of spidery headphones, fat clumsy dictionaries. Eyes looking down the cliff face, if only when I spoke, bits didn't fall off my words. Drawing, carefully, methodically and correcting it later, adding more to the peaked cap, filling in slowly, in detail the face, the eyes. Wobbly lists, hardly there at all really, making room for the spaces in between.

"Why are you fighting? What's the point?"

"We just like it, just something to do." In the rain, the shadows seem to be washed away. When he has gone, we go on punching bulletproof serge, never hitting the face, just short of bleeding. Perched on the ramp outside thin classrooms, what if they too blew away or just collapsed under the weight of winter? We can only hope. There was that storm wasn't there, last year, really frightened me, I hid though don't tell anyone. And: *"'What if there isn't anything after death? What then?"*

"Don't be stupid; of course there isn't any God. There wouldn't be any death would there? There wouldn't have been a Hitler." Beyond the skies there could be anything. All those stories and terrifying dreams take us above clouds and onto planets called heaven and hell. Bridges across Jupiter. Raging storms of words. If only I could write like that, if only I could be the first to walk on new hills or climb into the stars and name them. And oh, yes, we could breathe in strange worlds and even if they didn't speak English, we would manage, we would invent things, know things without being told.

> *In the forest there are always new things. I should know, I put them there. When you stay very quiet, just behind that tree eaten away with age and air and the slow grind of honey scented fungus and steely lichen. There's a gap. Bands of light. You can't miss it. What can you see? Who knows where the water comes from. It might have made itself, might have always been there.*

"You will have to say something, but who knows what." Nothing ready, nothing prepared. At the front of the room, behind a lectern, a TV news presenter with a smile ten yards wide invents a teacher in silkily poised description. Achievement after achievement glide through the loudspeakers. I know that, except for those who have already got their prizes, in everyone's minds are silent voices: 'This cannot be true," or *"This is not me."* I feel the words home in on me.

Earlier, the radio interviewer asked me what I would get if I won. I said I didn't know but possibly some sort of hat. There had been an appeal just before my interview: "Give us back our wheelchairs, the hospital can't keep replacing them." I spoke about the future of education. I said things were looking up. The interviewer looked me straight in the eyes and asked me what sort of hat it might be.

Afterwards, as I left, I heard the weather girl smooching with the interviewer, flirting with stormy fronts.

If I could, I would tame this chained heart. But it seems to belong now to someone else or something else. It has a life and aggressive vigour I do not recognize. I keep expecting people to say, put your heart away, it's too upsetting, too obvious.

There are huge screens with enlarged handwritten testimonials from parents and children about other teachers: *'Things were never the same again,'* *'I am a new person thanks to ...'* *'I have been given so much confidence.'* Building a better tomorrow with the Lloyds/TSB Bank. Tiny, tiny pastries vanish slowly.

There is no escape. Too many fictions have spun themselves around me from the podium to where I sit. So I look around for some words that might help. I know I must mean something. Big fat, purring words loiter on the platform to which I walk with uncertain, light tread. Smug words, words that know they are important, like someone's fantastically rich but abhorrent cousins brought round because they are impressive and One Ought To Learn Something From Their Manners. 'Of the Year.' 'In The West Midlands.' 'Award' and perhaps most ironic, 'Winner.'

If I could, I would run, both towards the bright lights and away from them, back into the foyer with cups of tea and warm, purple wine and dull, secure, lighting from unblinking, politely averted spotlights. Brittle talk there too but at least I sort of knew the script and could join in with the frightened joking of my friends.

But here, with my heart bouncing me up and down on my chair -

It's such a long walk up the hill and away from the school. Blood red houses with empty sightless windows. Was it here? Where did this start? Later a field gets turned over and in its place, a beautifully flat roofed square gets built out of glass and light. A pit of nettles lurks beneath the railings into which I saw my sister fall and disappear completely one day. *Go on, you know it, you know the answer.* Standing for so long thinking, wondering why there was a German boy in our class when we had won the war. *You know this; you've done this thousands of times.* And thinking: where is it ever safe? Words can bite you if you don't dress them up well, or make them right. Stinging, sudden pain if they get jumbled up and if you don't know why. Well, that just serves you right. *It's in there somewhere, you just have to look, you just have to think.*

Outside, even the rain seems to know better than us. It is a cold gang, ambushing and making play impossible for all but the very brave, us of course, who chase and tag and hide in places we make safe.

But in the kingdom of glass, there is no rain. Almost too much sunshine, in great drifts, apparently left here for us to play in and dress up in. Light which opens up the playing fields to dreams.

'I don't think it's about happiness.' Some walls are really thin, you wonder why they stand up or hold a roof on. In here we make sense of fictional lives, standing as anguished parents or lonely children, a foot nearer or a hand turned five or ten degrees downwards and the entire history of this family would be different, would almost become someone else's lives. Not a sound as we stand still, as we are inspected, moved round. Then a question: 'What has your son done to you? Why can't you patch things up?' And you find a voice which belongs to no one but comes to live here as naturally, as easily as if it was the same voice we use for shopping, bringing tea to loved ones, asking if this seat is taken. It hardly matters what I reply. The words are bags made of air and gentle intent, so gentle, they can be filled with bright and dark pictures by whoever listens or by no one.

In the shop, there is so much darkness. Fat bottles, like space helmets, filled with hundreds of bright lights, tower above and glow in the shadows. Wooden floorboards soft and spongy under foot. Behind the counter from where she has stepped out of every storybook we have ever read, an old and lonely witch takes our money and tells us not to make a mess of things. She is ten feet tall and as wide as a house. Her eyes have been borrowed from a shark. Some days she is a wolf and others she isn't there at all, but only a sound of a door being locked or window bolted or the sudden intake of breath before a scream. But this shop cannot be passed. We are infected by necessity and made brave by our friendships. Liquorice is all very well, but it is the chance it may be the last we ever buy which makes us enter this cave made of sherbet and night and lazy, dormant spells.

There are so many streets to walk down before we get to our Temperance Hall, the scaly green dragon at the top of the hill, it wouldn't be so bad if it spat fire, at least we'd be warm or the whole street would burst into flames and we'd get an unexpected holiday. But I suppose the air is too damp for that, too loaded with shadowy secrets to wake the creature. Its jaws are just open, still, and dark and we walk inside without a word, without complaint. There's as much trust as fear. In our pockets with the glassy eyed marbles and broken pencils are huge cartwheel pennies big enough to escape on if only we'd thought about it.

Sums like thickets. They can't be walked through. They just attack you. Not always while you're doing them. No, I'm happily getting answer after answer, making the division sign mean add up any number on the page. Why should it belong to just the two numbers either side of it, they might be only numbers you don't pay any attention to. So I don't. Or I do, or I work with only one of them, whichever of them can be divided by two or by folding the page or by forgetting about them altogether and wondering instead why yellow jumpers are so huge and seem to have a voice of their own if you listen carefully, lying in a slow sleepy heap in the corner by the table by the green box bubbling over with massive plastic bricks.

There are too many lights. They seem to be making the room darker. The TV newsreader bought in for the day to hand over the prizes, murmurs, "Well done, Graham." I trip over his smile. Another dignitary shakes my hand. A photo is taken and I just realize that this is, after all, happening to another me in another universe when a microphone materializes itself in the air in front of me. Words form, for myself I think, except that, alarmingly, I hear my voice, cosseted breathily round the room. "I don't know why the children are still in the room with me at the end of the lesson. I can't imagine why I've got this."

Just wait there for the present. It's weighing me down, this squat pillar of glass with my name etched in white, trapped on the surface beneath the sage, frozen profile of Plato. It might as well be Pluto.

There are faces far away. But they are in a dream, it doesn't seem to matter what happens, what I say, what I do.

> *You just go on through the trees, past the bunches of fist-like fungi. ' What have I told you? Watch where you tread, you know this isn't your sort of thing.' But who said anything about choice? When you're out here, that's just where you are, lost or not, you can't uninvent the forest. Shards of cold sunlight cut the air into fragments.*

The adjectives are taught. They are brought down from the attic and allowed bread and water before being sent back again, into the dark. "By the end of the lesson, you will be adjective experts. There are three paths towards this." I draw a pen on the board and words cluster round it, a little shame faced, a little uncertain, like guests at a party who have yet to be introduced. Their paper seems only half formed, not yet fully made, still part of the tree. It flutters under their fingers as if only fire would render it useful, not ink, not words. But out of the air they come, the inky stains. "How do you spell *exhilarating?*" "How do you spell car?" *It doesn't matter what they look like, just get them down, enjoy them, and want them.* But that's all right from where I stand, safely enough with the badges and tattoos of each hurdle and ditch successfully jumped. So, Jamie carves out the letters, as if inventing each one. Jeremy uses his book to attack the pen.

I take them to the computer room and their shadows dance across the silver screen. They make their words two feet high and project them onto the wall, words made out of granite or uncut diamonds or pure fire surge out of corners, creep into existence from nowhere, fragment and join, zoosh, laser or chatter in a typewriter sound they cannot recognize. Turning, twisting words, becoming three and two dimensional with a click and tap. Words you could build a house with scatter and then dance in front of you shamelessly.

I have a new scheme to help them relate to one another. They receive a nomination towards a star award each lesson they use phrases of politeness. They can also be rewarded for star listening. Stefan: "Before star awards came along everything was: link break link break link break." "And now?" "Now it's: link link link link." The inspector has no idea what Stefan means till she asks. "We are all linked together now. Before, the chain kept breaking."

Marie tells us that stars glow in the dark, they spin and they are very cold even though they are so hot. Did we know that? She says: "I didn't need to have a lesson on that. I already know about it all."

Weights are added to a spring which stretches down to the ground. The children watch intently. The spring is measured and the difference calculated. The children get into groups and try to do the same. All round the room, metal disks leap, rise, fall, and thump the benches. The distances are measured. "Two hundred centimeters." "No, millimetres, they're millimetres." The bell goes. Afterwards the teacher writes a note to me: *I can find nothing positive to say about these students. Nothing positive at all.*

You can trust some writing, like a parent, hold its hand, know what it's talking about even though you have no idea what the words mean or what's going on when they are strung together. And just sometimes, these words are your own, stumbled across, found lying around; perhaps even half mad, half formed. A story in a drawer, a poem you forgot to finish and now sitting half-dressed a little embarrassed as if slightly relieved it never got taken to a threatened party but still a little pleased with itself.

They can be very pleased with themselves and not want to have anything changed or tarted up. And they can pretend to be other people. Sometimes, in a policy document, they can strut around the page like secret policemen who want to be recognized. So many words have it within them to enjoy arrogance, like 'standards' 'rigour' 'performance.'

I say: "I want to see signs stuck above every classroom door reading *What Have You Learned Today?* Flipcharts in classrooms with lesson possibilities listed. And real talk about what happened in the last forty-five minutes and what difference it made to everyone." Time is so short, so short. I can feel these words sort of hobbling around, in the wrong clothes, uncertain where they belong but having to dress up because that's what it said on the invitation.

There are pretend faces all around, some nodding, and some clouding over. Papers, biscuits, coffee stains on the table. Crinkly overheads bake in the light of the one-eyed machine. Neat boxes and outcomes, objectives, arrows and timelines fracture the white wall. The air gets more and more stale and heavy. One or two people make eye contact and look away suddenly or furtively glance at each other, hoping either to signal alliance or difference, or command. Sometimes people get their looks ever so slightly wrong and unwittingly offer some unintended liaison which might just happen.

The French teacher uses space in her room as a prize, invites children into it, invites words and phrases to perform. Nowhere is off stage. There is a clatter of applause and smiles spread easily across faces. Outside, a ragged wind bounces across the playing fields: the teacher points through the window and coaxes guesses, half sentences and stumbling accents into the air. I want to join in, but I have a clipboard. Umbrellas, a slight chill and glimpses of the sun from behind a cloud.

Yes it's dark here sometimes. When it rains, it sounds like the whole forest is made of glass and shatters all over the place, all around you. And when it snows, you hardly dare breathe for fear of waking the giant. It's a strange place but it invented me and I don't mind it so much, knowing that. I tell people, it's all right here, and you don't need to worry about the shadows or the night because there are pathways all over the place really. You just have to make them and leave them and make them again.